Fifty Years of Family Voices

Fifty Years of Family Voices

THE STORY OF FAMILY FUND 1973–2023

Dr Chris Hanvey

Fifty Years of Family Voices: The Story of Family Fund 1973–2023

© Family Fund, 2023

Family Fund is hereby identified as the author of this work in accordance with the *Copyright, Designs and Patents Act 1988*.

A CIP record for this book is available from the British Library.

ISBN 9781908779618

Published by Step Beach Press, Hove BN3 2RE.

This book is published in association with Family Fund.

A catalogue record for this book is available from the British Library.

Written by Chris Hanvey

Edited by Jo Hathaway

Cover design and layout by Step Beach Press

Printed by L&S Printing Co Ltd, West Sussex, England

Dedicated to all of the children and families
whose lives have been improved by Family Fund,
and to the people who made that possible.

Contents

Acknowledgements

This book would not have been possible without the help of many supportive people. Re-engaging with Family Fund, after an absence of several years, was a reminder of what a special and warm 'family' it is – a word that is sometimes also used by carers.

Firstly, my thanks and unbounded admiration go to the families who, on top of school runs, looking for odd socks or school kit, found time to talk to me about Family Fund. Especially to Anne Donnelly, Claire Donnelly, Amanda Grist, Mandy Murphy and Jo Spear.

To Family Fund staff, still finding their way around hybrid working and patiently responding to yet more demands on their time: Claire Locker, Salena Begley, Ann Bond, Janice Foxton, Ben Calverley, Daniel Macheta, Roz Walton, Kate Fleck, Phil Henderson, Andrew Harper and Richard Hughes. It is invidious to single out people for special praise, but additional thanks to Elaine Pilmoor who kept me supplied with source material and negotiated visits to the Borthwick Institute for Archives, the University of York and Family Fund's CEO, Cheryl Ward, who has been both supportive and encouraging from inception to delivery.

To Trustee and previous Vice Chair David Braybrook who was always at the end of a telephone and provided invaluable advice, especially in relation to education and was my link with the Trustee board.

To Dame Christine Lenehan who, again, provided helpful information and is a long-time supporter and former trustee of Family Fund.

To Neil Adams, Archivist at the Borthwick Institute for Archives, the University of York.

To Derek Walpole, former CEO of Family Fund and a source of invaluable information.

To Dr Karen Horridge, Consultant Paediatrician (Disability) at South Tyneside and Sunderland NHS Foundation Trust and was invaluable in helping with data about medical advances for children.

To my wife Rosie, who has lived with boxes of source material all over the house and the clutter in my mind as I sought to provide a coherent account of this amazing organisation.

Chris Hanvey

Forewords

I would like to commend and congratulate Family Fund for reaching their 50th anniversary milestone.

I've long appreciated and admired the work of Family Fund. On a number of occasions as a constituency representative I've witnessed up close the real impact the organisation has made to the lives of families as they strive to meet the additional challenges of raising disabled and seriously ill children.

The gratitude I have for Family Fund is something I carried on when I was appointed Minister of Health in 2020 and I was very pleased to be able to subsequently announce a further in-year funding allocation which in turn helped many hundreds of families across Northern Ireland.

At this time of real pressure on household budgets the role of Family Fund has perhaps never been so important. On behalf of the countless young people and families across Northern Ireland that have been supported by it, I'd like to congratulate the organisation on reaching this anniversary and wish it every continued success for the future in undertaking its incredibly important and impactful work.

Robin Swann MLA, *Former Minister of Health in Northern Ireland*

The Scottish Government is delighted to join Family Fund in celebrating their 50th anniversary. Family Fund has a proud history of providing responsive, flexible support to families and carers with seriously ill and disabled children and young people in Scotland and is dedicated to understanding and addressing the challenges involved. I would like to pay tribute to all those involved for their hard work and commitment over the past 50 years.

Natalie Don MSP, *Minister for Children, Young People and Keeping the Promise, Scottish Government*

I would like to congratulate Family Fund for reaching their 50th anniversary milestone. The fund has a proud history of providing responsive, flexible support to families and carers with seriously ill and disabled children and young people across the United Kingdom. It is dedicated to really understanding and addressing the challenges families experience.

The UK Government is delivering for disabled people – in just the last year, we have supported the passage of two landmark pieces of legislation: the *British Sign Language Act* and the *Down Syndrome Act*. But this is no time to stand still. That is why we will be setting out, and consulting on, a Disability Action Plan over the course of this year. Our new action plan will be part of our commitment to create a society that works for everyone, where all can participate and be fully included.

This vision can only be achieved by working with expert organisations like Family Fund and with those with lived experience of disability. Family Fund's work is incredibly important and impactful and I wish the fund continued success for the future.

Tom Pursglove MP, *Minister of State for Disabled People, Health and Work of the UK*

As Permanent Secretary for Health, I am aware of the important work that Family Fund does in supporting with a grant, families with children who are living with a disability or serious illness in Northern Ireland. I understand fully what this grant support means to those families, particularly given the challenges they faced during the COVID-19 pandemic and those arising from the cost of living. I would like to take this opportunity to thank everyone at Family Fund for their hard work over many years in providing support to as many families as possible in Northern Ireland. In addition, I would like to congratulate Family Fund on achieving the very significant milestone of their 50th anniversary.

Peter May, *Permanent Secretary, Northern Ireland Department for Health*

I am delighted to hear Family Fund has reached their 50th anniversary of providing support for families of seriously ill children and young people across Wales and the wider UK. We know that families in Wales raising disabled or seriously ill children face substantial additional pressures and challenges in their lives. Thank you for all of the work that you do and the difference you have made and continue to make, in supporting and improving the lives of our families, children, and young people.

Many congratulations on achieving 50 years of much needed support for families across Wales.

Julie Morgan MS, *Deputy Minister for Social Services, Wales*

The Family Fund Trust have done incredible work in supporting children and young people with Special Educational Needs and Disabilities, and their families, over the course of their 50-year history. This book is a wonderful commemoration of all they have achieved.

Claire Coutinho MP, *Parliamentary Under-Secretary of State (Department for Education)*

Introduction

I have been involved with Family Fund since the early 1980s when I was a young social worker working with families in London. Its practical approach to supporting families with the basics of life was important then and it's important now. In the 2000s I also had the pleasure of being a Trustee at Family Fund for six years and was able to witness first-hand how it had grown and developed into a service which put families and young people at the heart and kept up to date with changing family needs. The data and research element of Family Fund is also able to give us a rich evidence base about the lives of families and is a key contributor to making change happen.

Dame Christine Lenehan, *DBE, Director, National Children's Bureau*

Family Fund has a special place in the heart of many who have had the privilege to lead the organisation over the last 50 years. Reading this book, researched and written by Dr Chris Hanvey, one of our former Trustees, has reminded me of the scale of change over the whole 50 year lifespan of the organisation. Although the differences are great between the political, social and technological environment in which the charity was founded in 1973 and the environment in which we now operate, the core ethos of the organisation remains the same as it was on Day One. Our vision is that families raising a disabled or seriously ill child have the same choices, quality of life, opportunities and aspirations as other families, and the determination to work towards this has been evident throughout our history. As Chris alludes to in the book, the future will bring more challenges for the families we support and for the team at Family Fund delivering that support, but we have a strong history to build on to continue our role of Being There for Families. I hope you enjoy the book and take the opportunity to learn more about the families we help and the history of an organisation that has for fifty years provided practical support to families at a time they needed it the most. My thanks to Chris for dedicating his time to delve into the last fifty years, and all the incredible people who have made Family Fund the organisation it is today.

Cheryl Ward, *Group Chief Executive, Family Fund*

A note on terminology

During a half century Family Fund has always been sensitive to those applying for assistance and has become steadily more nuanced in the way information on, say, disabilities, is recorded. Of course, language has changed and evolved over those fifty years. This is true not only in describing social class or income, but also in finding a language for minority ethnic groups, differences between the four nations (particularly post devolution) and variations in rates of applications across England, Scotland, Northern Ireland and Wales. Also, in terms of recording types of disability, definitions have both changed and become more thoughtful. Sometimes, in the book, reference is made to specific reports or publications and here the classifications of the time at which the date was recorded have been used.

How disability is defined by Family Fund

It is important to state the definition of disability upon which Family Fund has settled. It takes as its starting point what is often referred to as the 'social model of disability'. The child must have additional complex needs or a serious or life-threatening illness. These needs must affect the family's choices and opportunity to enjoy an ordinary life and the degree of planning and support must be much greater than that usually required for children and young people. The condition must be long term or life limiting and the carers must require a high level of support in some of the following areas: the physical environment, education, communication, access to social activities, personal care and supervision.

The voice of families

The story of Family Fund is brought alive by the thousands of families who have been supported by its grants over the fifty years since its founding. Their voices are scattered throughout the book but details, including names, have been changed. Only the longer transcripts, sandwiched between the chapters, and where permission has been granted, contain real names.

Generally, in the text, the Joseph Rowntree Memorial Trust or Foundation is referred to as 'JRF'.

Chapter 1

Philanthropy With A Very Human Face

Back in 1973 the fashion was for big hair, tie-dye shirts, bell bottom trousers and clogs. Cliff Richard was to take part in the Eurovision Song Contest (coming third), Slade, Donny Osmond and Gilbert O'Sullivan were Top of the Pops and the first handheld mobile phone – as large as a medium size brick – was launched. Edward Heath was the Prime Minister and, in January, the UK joined the-then-European Economic Community.

That same year a 12-year-old girl in Wales had to attend a hospital in London for treatment and an operation on 9th April for a 'cardiac abnormality'. The local authority social services department were prepared to pay the mother's costs to travel with her daughter and only child, but this did not include expenses to enable her husband to accompany them. The family lived on a low income and, understandably, the father was keen to be with his family. On April 2nd an application was submitted to the very newly established Family Fund to allow him to travel to his family and, on the following day, a cheque for £26 was sent, to allow the father to visit his daughter in hospital for three weekends, during the expected stay for the operation. The first grant was duly recorded at the top of a brand-new ledger and Family Fund was in operation. As the Committee of the Joseph Rowntree Foundation, who approved the grant, later noted:

> "This was a good example of the Fund being used to complement the services of the local authority."
> Second meeting of the new board on 17th April 1973

This very first entry can still be seen in the ledger, held in Borthwick Institute for Archives in the University of York, and right at the top. By June of the same year the ledger was beginning to fill with, amongst other things, an application for unbreakable glasses, a specially-made saddle for a boy with no arms intent on horse riding and a sewing machine for a mother to make clothes. Family Fund was beginning to fulfil its promise, made in the *Times Education Supplement* of 30th March, 1973 that this was to be a fund with 'a very human face'. Yet who could possibly know that this was to represent the first of hundreds of thousands of grants, and millions of pounds, which would go on to be awarded for the next fifty years, to families of disabled children across the whole of the UK. Grants awarded by Family Fund which, slightly echoing the comment from the *Times Educational Supplement*, developed a reputation for efficiency and friendliness:

> "I tried Family Fund and they were fantastic. There was no hanging about, they just got on with it."
> A parent

Fiftieth birthdays and anniversaries are very special; usually recognised with gold and representing an ability to have weathered whatever is thrown in the way. This is certainly true of Family Fund. It is a remarkable story beginning, as we have just seen, with the recording of a grant in a large ledger probably not very different from the way applications from destitute people under the 19th Century Poor Law were recorded and continuing to the present development of accessible software. This not only encourages interaction through on-line applications but supports those who are digitally excluded, whilst at all times making possible the building of an unrivalled database of knowledge and understanding of the needs of disabled children and their families.

As well as the relatively minor challenges of evolving technology, Family Fund has lived through devolution in the UK, a transformation of the voluntary sector across the UK and huge changes in the way education and health care are delivered, the growth of the private social care sector and periodic attempts to reform the welfare benefits system. Across social care, Family Fund began supporting the newly established social work departments and today continues to complement the provision of support. Two factors are particularly noticeable as a backcloth against which Family Fund has operated: the growth of the voluntary sector and the periodic attempts to reform welfare benefits.

As far as the voluntary sector is concerned, it has undergone not one but two transformations in the last fifty years. With the establishment of local authority social services departments in the early 1970s it looked as if the voluntary sector would be reduced to a minor role on the stage, fitting in around an increasingly important system of state intervention. As demand for services increased and the local authority incomes were cut, however, the voluntary sector was revitalised, applying, in some cases, for grants and contracts to supplement what the state was providing. And, of course, the offer of additional voluntary sector funds to run these services was particularly welcome to stretched local authorities. With this growth of charities came a flexing of muscles from a sector which, because of its growth, had become able to speak truth to power. Alongside direct services, the voluntary sector increased its influencing and lobbying, pressing for changes, publishing research it commissioned itself and using the media to raise awareness and often campaign on behalf of disadvantaged groups. An understanding of this development is important when placed against the way Family Fund has evolved in the last half century. As we shall see, it has developed from grant maker to influencer of the way support could be offered to families of disabled children.

An even bigger backcloth has been the evolution of welfare benefits. Reference to some of the major changes are made throughout the book. As we see throughout, Family Fund has consistently worked to enhance state support, working in conjunction with other organisations and, on one occasion in 1987, being invited to take on a part of the welfare benefits system. This, even more than the evolution of the voluntary sector, has been subject to the vagaries of political ideology. Seen at its most simplistic, the fifty years can be characterised by the ebb of increasing state assistance followed by the flow of tighter control of financial support, constraining expenditure and motivated by financial crises or political ideology. Navigating through this – and in an increasing four nation context – has been one of the major challenges and triumphs of Family Fund.

What has not changed has been the constancy of the four UK governments in continuing to contribute grant funding to Family Fund. Originally, this grant funding was from the Department of Health and Social Security on behalf of all four countries. However, with devolution, came separate negotiations with Wales, Scotland and Northern Ireland. With this has come the evolution of Family Fund in different ways. As we shall see, devolution allowed the freedom for separate initiatives which, in some cases, represented differing political priorities. Again, as we shall later see, the triumph of Family Fund has been to evolve differently, maintaining a 'local' context and reflecting the needs of the nations, whilst not being seen as an English organisation with little sensitivity to the rest of the UK.

This is, at one level, the narrative of a remarkable organisation. But more importantly than this it is the story of a remarkable group of parents, carers and their children whose resilience, supported by Family Fund, shines through. Hopefully, their voices can be heard throughout the book. They are ordinary people doing remarkable things, caring and bringing up their children, by definition, on low incomes but determined to give their families the same range of opportunities and experiences that other families enjoy. Often time-poor, they are nevertheless ceaseless in fighting for what their children need and deserve. You need look no further than the words of carers about the family breaks that have become such an important element of Family Fund's grants. What these breaks have made possible has been the opportunity to create the same memories that other families can take for granted. Lastly, what has also characterised Family Fund has been the constant willingness to listen; to build the grant-making programme around what carers need and, in the latter years, to develop programmes and services in direct response to the concerns of parents and carers. As you might expect from this, Family Fund's vision is of an 'inclusive society, where families with disabled or seriously ill children have the same choices and opportunities as other families to enjoy ordinary life'.

Anne, two generations of Family Fund, 1980–2023

I am visually impaired. I was born prematurely so my retinas didn't develop properly. I went to a special school, because I would not have been able to cope with simple things like reading the blackboard. From there I went on the Royal National College in 1979 where I learnt touch typing and Braille shorthand. I later trained to work with both adults and children with visual impairments.

I have four children, the oldest of whom, Kizzy, is the only one without a visual impairment. The children had congenital cataracts and have needed lots of surgery which, over the years, we have dealt with.

I first became involved with the charity Home-Start and the lady who visited asked if I had heard of Family Fund. Through a referral we were then able to get help and we had several family holidays, made possible through Family Fund grants. They were wonderful holidays. Money was very tight; we had hard times and could not otherwise have afforded to go on holiday. They let us do things we couldn't do at home. The children went rock pooling with my husband, discovering creatures in the shallow water, collecting seaweed and generally exploring. We had ice creams and enjoyed all the things that were different from being at home.

On one holiday I had a guide dog and we all went paddling. The dog saw I had gone into the sea and thought I needed to be rescued. Paws were put on my shoulder and we all ended up sitting, with our clothes on in the sea. Everyone on the beach was laughing. On one holiday in Norfolk we went on a steam train. My husband is an engineer and could explain the engine to the children who were intrigued.

In Scotland we had a cottage in the middle of nowhere. I think we must have been near a farm and the cows managed to escape. There they were, looking into the cottage through the windows. On that same holiday we visited a family-run theme park, which the children particularly enjoyed. Once they had paid the entrance fee they could wander where they wanted and go on the rides. We took a blind friend of mine with us – she paid for her own holiday – and the children persuaded her to go on a ride, which they said would be gentle. She ended up being spun and turned upside down and my husband couldn't work out if she was going to cry. When she came off, she asked if they could do it all over again – and the children still speak fondly of the day they took Auntie Elaine on the Magic Swinging Sword!

On one holiday the children wanted to dissect and eat a crab. We went to a fish shop where they chose their cooked crab and came back and had great fun taking it apart and talking about it. And, of course, they were able to go back to school and tell their friends that they had been on holiday.

One year, with a Family Fund grant, we went by car to Cornwall, which was a very long drive. It was the hottest day of the year and there had been an oil slick on the motorway. There were huge queues. Near us a toddler was put by the side of the road with the potty and we started to make friends with everyone around us. A lorry driver, in a huge cab, was higher than us and would tell us if the road was clearing. Amongst the children food was swapped and a number of sandwiches exchanged for generous quantities of After Eight mints. When we were in the car we always sang the whole of the time. We also took the children to a water mill, where they could see the corn being ground and enjoyed simple things like feeding the ducks.

The holidays were different from a humdrum existence, and they brought much anticipation and a real bit of joy. We looked forward to them all year. They sustained us throughout the year and helped us forget work and just enjoy being together as a family.

Family Fund is fantastic and has now helped my daughter – so it has moved to the next generation. It has been a life saver, giving us an opportunity to escape the stress of everyday life. In my professional life, running the sensory services in Orkney, I have referred others to Family Fund when it seemed appropriate.

Keep up the good work!

Chapter 2

'A Remedy Of Proven Value'*

*(The Cohen Committee)

Thalidomide

It was hailed as a wonder drug. Between 1958 and 1961 pregnant women who reported morning sickness were prescribed thalidomide. It was marketed as a sedative which, reputedly had none of the side effects of barbiturates. Originally, it was from Germany, produced by Chemie Grunenthal and manufactured in the UK by the Distiller Company (Biochemical) Ltd. What was originally not known was that thalidomide, while reducing morning sickness, anxiety and lack of sleep, was a 'teratogen', meaning that it disturbed the development of the embryo and led to birth defects. If taken between the fourth and sixth week of pregnancy, thalidomide often led to children being born with significant disabilities.

In the UK at that time over four hundred children were affected, and, across the world, this figure rose to over 10,000. The government's own drug safety advisers, the Cohen Committee, had declared that thalidomide was safe ('a remedy of proven value') and between 1960 and 1963 Enoch Powell, the Minister of Health, sought to distance himself from a gathering storm of parents and carers. He refused to help the families, rejected an inquiry into the origins of the disaster and was not prepared to set up a drug testing centre which would seek to prevent a similar reoccurence. The parents were left with little option but to seek redress through the courts and bring an action for damages.

In August 1962, sixty-two of the families began a civil action. Fortunately, Sir Harold Evans had first come across some of the families when he was editor of the **Northern Echo** and before he moved to the **Sunday Times**. By 1967 not one of the families had received a penny in compensation and the government was faced with an increasing dilemma. On the one hand was a sustained and successful **Sunday Times** campaign, under the banner of 'Our Thalidomide Children, Cause for National Shame', galvanising the public; on the other, there was a determination to ensure that what was Distiller's responsibility to provide compensation, should not be settled by the British government (Evans, 2009).

By this time Sir Keith Joseph was the Secretary of State for Health and Social Security and faced an adjournment debate in 1972 in which the MP Jack Ashley urged the government to 'establish a fund for the children, immediately without prejudice to present negotiations'.

As both parliamentary and national interest increased, so too did the idea of a special fund which would both support families and accept the responsibility the state had for distributing a damaging drug. However, even with this public pressure, Sir Keith Joseph was cautious. Debates as to whether the government had a general responsibility to pay compensation to anybody who had suffered any injury or damage resulting from the use of any drug which had been prescribed under the NHS still continued. Also, Sir Keith Joseph did not want to allow Distillers to avoid their responsibilities and, however much children affected by thalidomide needed assistance, there were other children with disabilities who were equally in need of support. There were, the Minister argued, three tests that should be addressed before any fund was set up. Firstly, that it did not prejudice a settlement with Distillers. Secondly, that it did not leave out other severely disabled children, and, thirdly, that help given to families affected by thalidomide would complement support from local authorities and statutory provision. On 29th November 1972 and under pressure from the public, families and the *Sunday Times*, Sir Keith Joseph announced to Parliament that a fund would be established 'to ease the burden of living on those households containing very severely congenitally disabled children' (*House of Commons Debates*, vol. 847, col. 4980.) Initially, £3 million was to be provided, with more help to follow when the litigation was settled. It was not to be seen as compensation but to complement the services already provided by statutory and voluntary bodies.

Once the idea of a fund had been agreed, there was considerable debate in the national press. Should it be an independent trust? How would it fit in alongside state benefits? How wide would the net for recipients be cast? A number of options presented themselves. The first was that the fund should be administered by the government's Supplementary Benefits Commission but this was hard pressed, as was the Attendance Allowance Board – another option. An alternative was to give the administration of a fund to local authorities. They had recently, in 1970, assumed responsibilities for the *Chronically Sick and Disabled Person's Act* and it was beginning to show how difficult it was for local authorities to maintain equivalent standards. Local authorities were also fully engaged in other directions. Just prior to the General Election in 1970, parliament had passed the *Social Services Act* and the newly formed social work departments were focussed on establishing themselves. This, on top of the *Chronically Sick Act* and the Attendance Allowance, also introduced in 1970, left little space for the administration of a new grant. The other option was an entirely new trust but this would have taken both time to set up and also entirely new legislation. If, however, it was possible to align with an existing charity this would fit in with the Conservative philosophy of voluntary rather than government action, particularly as no government department felt able to take on the administration.

On November 30th 1972 the Department of Health and Social Security contacted the Joseph Rowntree Memorial Trust to ask if they, or a similar large trust, would consider running such a fund. The JRF was seen as a credible national organisation, with links into other national networks. On 6th December 1972, the Department of Health and Social Security followed this up with a meeting with the Joseph Rowntree Memorial Trust at Alexander Fleming House, expressing the view that they were seeking an organisation which would be 'reliable, efficient and discreet'.

In 1904 Joseph Rowntree, a Quaker, philanthropist, businessman and owner of a chocolate factory in York, established the Joseph Rowntree Village Trust and in 1959 this had been re-born as the Joseph Rowntree Memorial Trust. Its primary work was to deploy a substantial income in housing and social research. It had no direct experience of running a trust and administering funds to families, as was being proposed by the government. The Trust was not staffed for such an enterprise and this would be a very new departure in their public administration. There was also a strong underlying feeling that this could be a small step in a much bigger initiative to help families, but at the same time a concern remained that the Trust could be linked, in the public's mind, to the previous poor treatment of families affected by thalidomide.

The Trustees of JRF deliberated hard before reaching a decision. As was remarked at the time, never before had six people taken so long to accept £3 million. The Trustees knew that there was little real evidence of either the numbers or the needs of children with significant disabilities and the national controversy that thalidomide had attracted could, it was argued, rebound on the Trust itself. There was also the immediate challenge of helping potentially large numbers of very deprived families. However, on the other side of the argument, involvement would assist the Trust in becoming involved in new areas of social policy, with very practical and positive outcomes.

Family Fund is born

In a paper written in 1979, Jonathan Bradshaw reflected back on a fund which was announced '*without clarity of purpose, with uncertainty about its clientele and with little or no consideration of how it would operate or its*

long-term implications'. Nevertheless, the JRF board eventually agreed to go ahead, to receive the first £3 million, and to set up a Fund as a subsidiary of the Joseph Rowntree Trust. They did, however, set a number of conditions which were both important and subsequently guided the way Family Fund, as it became known, was to operate. Firstly, the Trust could not act as an agent of government. It was prepared to negotiate broad guidelines but decisions about the allocation of individual grants would be by the trustees alone. Secondly, the administration of Family Fund should initially be confined to a three-year period and, lastly, there should be a gradual phasing of the introduction of Family Fund, so that the Trust could assess what resources would be necessary. Faced with these challenges and the difficulty of steering an independent course, one commentator at the time ruefully said, "How can the unfortunate Trust cope?" (Waddilove, 1983).

A letter from the Department of Health and Social Security to Lewis Waddilove, the Director of JRF, dated 21st December 1972, officially confirmed that JRF would assume responsibility for administering Family Fund. So, who was Family Fund aimed at helping? Firstly, the letter agreed, it was for families in England, Scotland, Wales and Northern Ireland with children under the age of 16 who are *'severely congenitally handicapped, whether physically (including the totally blind or deaf) or mentally'*. Sixteen was the cut-off point because, after that, children became eligible for financial support under the supplementary benefits system. Secondly, for those whose economic or social circumstances were such that they needed money, goods or services, in order to relieve *'stress on the family while the handicapped child is at home'* and which the Trustees would determine. As such, Family Fund would complement other statutory support from income maintenance or social services. The DHSS would pay the costs of administration and the agreement would be reviewed in three years' time. 'All' that remained was for the Trust to set up the administration and governance structure.

Of course, plenty of questions were unresolved: Would Family Fund prove sufficient? How would definitions around 'very severely' and 'congenitally handicapped' be decided? Furthermore, how was an independent trust to work in conjunction with statutory bodies, such as the newly formed social services departments?

Two fundamental points are vital to understanding the origins of the Family Fund. The first was the belief that there was a finite number of families who would apply to this new fund. Some early calculations by the Joseph Rowntree Trust, based on the number of 'severely handicapped' children as defined at the time, aged under 17 and living in the community in England and Wales, concluded that there were about 400 children affected by thalidomide, 4,500 with spina bifida, and 26,000 with 'severe mental sub normality', 7,000 with cerebral palsy, 500 with phenylketonuria and 100 with muscular dystrophy. A belief, reflected in a Joseph Rowntree minute of 2nd October 1975 records that

> 'It seemed that over the next year most of those eligible to apply to Family Fund would have done so and there should then be a reduction in the number of applications. This, together with the known drop in the birth rate of handicapped children, should result in substantial cuts in expenditure'.

Alongside the figures quoted above, the government's initial information was that the overall figure was less than 100,000 (Waddilove, as above). Based on a sample of children in York who were deemed severely disabled, Jonathan Bradshaw also calculated that figure to be between 74,000 and 102,000 families for the UK. This argument is reminiscent of the speculation which accompanied the setting up of the NHS in 1948. Once patients had received their free NHS glasses or false teeth, demand would gradually reduce. As we shall see, nothing could be further from the truth – as it was for the NHS! – and a vitally important part of Family Fund's history, during the next fifty years, was centred upon discovering the depth of unmet need.

An equally important point is the principle that has remained for fifty years. In no other situation has a privately managed Fund or other non-statutory body been given the task of distributing a substantial amount of Exchequer money. It was unprecedented in British social policy that a trust should distribute public money. In 1973 this was £3 million: by the end of March 2021 the combined income for Family Fund was over £55 million, albeit that this also included funding from other sources. It is doubtless the case that the Trustees' decision in December 1972 had a hugely positive impact on the lives of hundreds of thousands of families. As Lord Seebohm stated, writing a Foreword in Lewis Waddilove's book on the Joseph Rowntree Memorial Trust, and commenting on the early years of Family Fund, '*apart from teething troubles (it) has been a resounding success*' (Waddilove, 1983). The role and decision of the JRF Trustees has never been taken lightly. As early as 1975 the-then Director of the Joseph Rowntree Memorial Trust wrote to Professor Kathleen Jones acknowledging that '*the moral responsibility of the Trust here is very considerable*'.

The first meeting of the newly constituted Family Fund was held in York on 2nd February 1973. Mr Peter Barclay was appointed as Chairman of the Management Committee, Lord Seebohm, the Chair of the Joseph Rowntree Foundation became a member alongside Tom White, the Director of Social Services for Coventry, other representatives from the Trust and DHSS observers. Near the top of the agenda was finding someone to administer Family Fund. Fairly soon after the meeting Dennis Hitch, previously Assistant Director of Social Services, was appointed as the first Chief Executive of Family Fund, and in a later article published in the *Times Education Supplement* (30th March 1973) he promised that Family Fund would have a 'very human face', a pledge that has survived for fifty years. While some detractors were critical that Family Fund had been awarded to a voluntary provider – given that it was distributing statutory funding – the *Daily Express* wrote a positive article, pointing to some imaginative grants that had been made up to 1st August (see below).

From the date of the first grant in April 1973 until 1st August of the same year, applications were only accepted for children who had reached their tenth birthday and were not yet 16. This would allow JRF to recruit staff and not be overwhelmed by a number of applications too great for the organisation to process. The Trustees also took two significant actions which were to have a profound effect on the way that Family Fund was to develop: forging a research link with the University of York and establishing a medical advisory subcommittee.

Keeping a record of applications

From August 1973 it was agreed that there would be a record of each family applying to Family Fund which would, in time, create an unprecedented source of research data on Family Fund's work. JRF were keen, from the outset, to monitor the lessons learned both about the needs of the families and the stress they were experiencing, and the extent to which grants helped to relieve this. To this end a partnership was made with the University of York's Department of Social Administration and Social Work and the Family Fund project was born. The cost was shared between JRF and the Department of Health and Social Security which, in February 1974 agreed a grant of £53,500 to the University of York, over a period of four years. Not only was this one of the most successful research operations which JRF initiated but it established a precedent, maintained over 50 years, for evaluating the effectiveness of the Trust's work. Jonathan Bradshaw was appointed the research fellow and, in 1980, he published a book on the administration of Family Fund during the first three years of its existence.

The Family Fund databank took information from the social work form of families applying, coded it and put it onto a data file. It produced 'Trends in Applications' and, supported by the Research Advisory Group, the University of York became steadily more sophisticated in using Family Fund's data. It was an inspired piece of foresight and, as we shall see later, produced an unrivalled database on clinical, epidemiological, social and economic circumstances, related to families with a disabled child. It is a unique record, too, of the way that the profile of families has changed over 50 years.

The second significant action was the establishment of what became known as the Medical Advisory Panel. It will be recalled that before accepting responsibility for Family Fund, there was uncertainty as to what was meant by 'severely congenitally handicapped' and how a workable definition could be found to assist the applications. A good example of this was children with Down's syndrome which, in the early days of grants, exercised the Trustees. Originally, very young children with Down's syndrome were rejected. It was argued – and the same principle applied to other conditions affecting very young children – that all babies were in need of support and therefore it would be inappropriate to single out some help which, theoretically, applied to all babies.

The Fund called upon the advice of Ross Mitchell, Professor of Child Health at Dundee University who, with the help of other colleagues, tackled the challenge of defining what severe disability was and which conditions were defined as 'congenital'. This early work was to prove crucial for the whole evolution of Family Fund. There remained the lingering fear that JRF could be re-drawn into the original debates around thalidomide and what constituted severe disability.

Professor Mitchell convinced JRF that the severity of disability and not handicap should be the real test of eligibility. Disability, it was argued, could be more objectively assessed than handicap and allowed for the element of stress experienced by the family. It was the beginning of what we now refer to as the social model of disability, where proof of eligibility depends on an element of discretion and an holistic assessment of the effect that a particular condition has on the total circumstances of the family. This is explained in a Minute of Family Fund in May 1973 which declared firstly, that no form of means test should be employed and secondly, that when considering the level of income it was important to take into account how the child's disability impacted on the family's way of life, particularly in comparison with their peers.

From August 1st 1973 the criteria was widened to include children under ten and at the end of 1974 the word 'congenital' was dropped from the consideration of the disability. As Family Fund started feeling its way, early Board minutes record the kind of applications which were being received. In June 1973 there was a request for a specially made saddle for an 'armless' boy keen to take up horse-riding, and for unbreakable spectacles for a child who destroyed them all too easily. For a widowed mother of three children, two of whom had muscular dystrophy, Family Fund made a grant of £470 for the installation of central heating; a grant of £250 was given towards the construction of a separate room for a disabled boy and, as an indication, from the outset, of Family Fund's flexibility, the grant of a car. This latter application occupied debate within the Board. The mother, herself disabled, had three 'congenitally handicapped' children and needed more substantial transport than the Mini provided by the DHSS. Family Fund allowed her to change this for a more suitable vehicle, up to the value of £1,500. In these earliest days the biggest demand was for clothing, bedding, washing machines, cars and driving lessons.

Despite the grants described above, the uptake was slow and Family Fund questioned whether it was effectively communicating the scope of its help. On 1st August 1973 the Chair, Peter Barclay, issued a press release through the *Daily Mirror*, referring to the popular gossip and nosey parker in the soap *Coronation Street*, to attract some publicity:

> *'We need people like Ena Sharples who take an interest in what is going on in their street. They should inform neighbours that this money is available.'*

The message was clear – Family Fund was up and running and available to all disabled children under 16 and their families. During these first three years, Family Fund also used the PR firm, Forma House, to publicise its work more widely. While the Trustees were self-critical, a report in the *Daily Express*, on 1st August 1973 (referenced above) pointed to some imaginative grants and concluded that

> *'On the record of its first months' activities Family Fund sets an imaginative and humane example to the rest of the Welfare State.'*

Not surprisingly, a further grant of £3 million was made in 1974 and a later decision was taken to extend Family Fund for a further five years.

The early years

As Family Fund grew in confidence and the range of situations assessed widened, building up a body of precedent decisions and increased understanding, the Trustees agreed to set up an appeals panel for this discretionary fund, to decide on disputed decisions. Over a period of time the minutes record that Trustees adjudicated on decisions as diverse as transport, telephones, the use of some kinds of treatment and educational facilities. The assessments themselves were done by a range of professionals, such as health visitors, with the Trustees resisting the request that they should only be carried out by qualified social workers. Over a short period, a network of part-time workers were recruited, based across the country but reporting in to the JRF in York.

We know a lot about the first three years of Family Fund, because of Jonathan Bradshaw's account (Bradshaw, 1980). It is the story of an organisation keen to meet the needs of families in a transparent way and having to set up an administration from scratch, within the body of a Trust that was strong on social policy and research but which had little experience of engaging so directly with service users. We learn from this account that there were initially huge variations of applications between regions and that the Trustees were initially concerned with take up of grants. Bradshaw records that the largest 'handicapping condition' was then categorised as 'mental sub normality', followed by spina bifida and cerebral palsy and the largest group of applicants, according to the 1973 General Household Survey, was made up of manual workers. Bradshaw's research also revealed that only between a third and a half of those eligible for help had been notified to apply, that more work was needed to iron out inconsistencies and that, in terms of the emotional stress of looking after a child with a disability, Family Fund went some way to relieving the burden of care for many families.

Even from the outset, in 1972, there was a belief from the Trustees of JRF that it would be difficult to defend the withdrawal of support from families where the children had reached the age of 16. It is an argument which has been repeated, with Family Fund wishing to continue to offer support at least to those in that age group that needed help. As we shall see below, in 1986 there was a bid to extend the age limit up to 20 and, from 1984, Family Fund produced information for young people over the age limit of 16 on benefits and additional support made available from other sources. The ability to provide grant support for that age group was still to be secured.

Bradshaw's conclusions, after three years of Family Fund, was that 97% of grant recipients were pleased with the support offered. It was not unduly costly to administer, had been set up with very little criticism – despite the huge sensitivity and publicity around thalidomide and – 'was a very inexpensive form of provision' (Bradshaw, as above).

Does Family Fund continue?

A number of recurrent themes were to characterise the next few years, until another major change in 1996: uncertainty about the future of Family Fund; debates about the cut off point for eligibility; changes to social security arrangements; and fluctuating levels of funding. At a meeting of the Board in February 1975, it was agreed to continue Family Fund until 1978, with a feeling that, after this, the responsibility might be divided between a variety of governmental and non-governmental agencies. It was still seen as temporary and, as a minute of 2nd October 1975 recorded

> *'It seemed that over the next year most of those eligible to apply to Family Fund would have done so and there should then be a reduction in the number of applications'.*

Furthermore, a new cash benefit, the Mobility Allowance, was introduced in 1976, to assist with mobility needs through using taxis, mobility scooters etc, and which initially reduced the demand on Family Fund for transport. Another minute from the Board in June 1977 records that the government was unsure of future plans for Family Fund. There was talk of a supplementary Family Allowance or alternatively, part of the need might be met by a new laundry allowance, given that additional laundry was a considerable challenge for many families.

In 1978 the uncertainty continued, with five options being considered. The first of these was to continue Family Fund through JRF or another organisation, with a grant of something less than £2 million a year. The next was to bring Family Fund to an end, with no alternative provision proposed. Thirdly, and returning to the 1977 proposal, a specific grant, comparable to the newly introduced Mobility Allowance to resolve the problem of excessive laundry or, fourthly, a general allowance comparable to the Constant Attendance Allowance. Finally, there was the option of continuing the service but it being run either by local authorities or by the Supplementary Benefits commission. The conclusion was to continue Family Fund for the foreseeable future, making regular grants, committing to a three-year review and positioned alongside the statutory funding provided by welfare benefits. By June 1979 the minutes reveal that Family Fund had received applications from 51,000 families and distributed grants in cash or kind to the value of £14.5m. The point was being forcibly made that this new way of distributing government funding, using an existing Trust as the instrument (and a test of whether the giving of discretion to a voluntary agency might have advantages) demonstrated improved care and efficiency versus the direct distribution of grants through the government's own departments.

The dilemma over what happened next to Family Fund continued into the 1980s and is reflected in the Trustee Board minutes. It wasn't as if the government had started something they now wanted to finish but more that they realised they had developed something so useful that they didn't know which direction to take it. In 1980 there was a formal letter from the Director to the Department of Health and Social Security, recognising that it was unrealistic to continue to regard Family Fund as a temporary arrangement but that it had not as yet become a permanent institution.

Debates about the eligibility for those over 16 continued too. It was part of a much larger discussion about the transition from children to adult services for those with disabilities and a knowledge that, frequently, welfare benefits didn't fulfil some of the support that Family Fund had come to provide. So, in 1986, there was a debate by the Trustees recorded in the minutes that the age limit should be extended to the age of 20. Family Fund already had 14,000 young people who would be on their register aged 16–19 and qualifying for assistance. It was argued that, in some ways, a cut off at 20, rather than 16 was just as arbitrary but would at least help with this transition from children to adult services. Equally significant, by the mid-1980s public expenditure had slowed down and social security policy was increasingly aimed at constraining expenditure: the need for Family Fund was becoming even greater.

Supplementing the welfare state

Evidence of this shift in government policy was demonstrated by the 1985 Green Paper, 'Reform of Social Security' which pointed to the increasing costs of state benefits and proposed a framework for a new and simpler system of income-related help. It resulted in the *Social Security Act 1986* and, for Family Fund, a surge in new applications for some much-needed items where there was uncertainty as to whether statutory help would be available.

In the following year, 1987, Nicholas Scott, then Minister for the Disabled in the Department of Social Security, approached Family Fund with a plan for a new grant. Under what was argued to be a new simpler system of income support there would be a group of several hundred severely disabled people – living in their own homes – who, because of the new system, would be denied extra help. The government was looking at a longer term solution to address their needs and in the interim was prepared to put £5m in a new fund for three years to provide extra help. The Minister wrote on 23rd December to Family Fund asking whether the Trustees would be prepared to administer this proposal effectively to support this group for whom help would not be available within the parameters of the current social security system. Naturally, the proposal went to the Board of Trustees but it was turned down. The Trustees were very clear and their reasoning was important. In a letter of 19th January, back to the Department, they stated that:

Help that Family Fund provided was always to be 'in addition to support from central and local government'. It was this clarity that had permitted Family Fund to escape criticism, right from the outset, that it was an agent of government rather than an independent body providing support that would not be available from statutory sources.

As the 1980s gave way to the 1990s the volume of successful grants steadily grew. Family Fund had received its first word processor in 1981 and by 1992 all of the records were computerised. An independent review of Family Fund, conducted by Korda and Co. in 1985, called for a greater use of what was described as 'office technology' but was also fulsome in its praise. As the report concluded, 'the commitment is summed up by the setting of targets for responding to requests which few commercial organisations could match, let alone the Civil Service'.

> "I remember when we got our first word processor we thought, 'this is it – one person will do everything on the word processor and the rest of us will go'."
>
> Family Fund staff member

In 1994 Family Fund celebrated its 21st birthday with a publication by Alison Cowen entitled *Taking Care*. It recognised that since 1973 Family Fund had provided help to the families of approximately 120,000 children, as well as contributing significantly to research relating to services for families of children with a disability. One of the major strengths, as Cowen argues, is that it is families themselves who determine their needs. What is also very significant about this publication is that it is carers themselves who have written the book. It is by parents, for parents, and a collaboration between researchers, practitioners and carers. They talk, for example, about the stress they experience, their determination to have the same rights and opportunities as other families and the huge challenges of accessing services for their children. In many ways Family Fund had made another very significant leap forward in its coming of age. Not only had it established its independence from government, setting criteria for grants that were universally accepted, but it listened to parents and carers in a way that the deliverers of statutory welfare services rarely did. It was time for Family Fund to take another major step forward.

The 1990s: Amanda and son Ryan

Family Fund has been amazing. It is only now, when Ryan is an adult and I look back over his life, that I realise what support it gave.

Over the years, starting in the 1990s and continuing into the 2000s, we have been helped with holidays, days out, furniture and a computer. In the early years, when Ryan was small, money was tight and we could not have afforded these things.

I remember the very first year. I felt very nervous before we were visited by the Family Fund visitor. You don't like asking for anything. It's like admitting you can't cope. The support was very helpful. Occasionally Ryan would damage the furniture or his clothes – he would only wear certain types of clothes, so help here was much appreciated. Here was an organisation that would listen to us. The help continued until Ryan became 16.

The fact that someone listened was important. Ryan is autistic. When he was a boy autism wasn't understood. People didn't really believe in autism and just thought that he was badly behaved. People are more open now. They have begun to see the positive sides of autism and the way that these children are wired in a different way. Autistic people see things differently. Now there is more understanding. We're more open now. But not then.

Ryan has two siblings and the support Family Fund gave helped them as well. We went on Haven holidays which they enjoyed. Ryan liked his football, so it was important we found somewhere where he could play. And his brother and sister were also able to use the computer Family Fund provided.

The difficulty is that the benefits system is horrendous. It always makes you feel awful. The system really needs scrapping and starting again. The narrative is that you are a faker or a fraud and you have, somehow, to ride through this. Every time you had to reapply it was a battle. Ryan is partially sighted, his eyesight is never going to get better. But every two years we had to prove all over again that his sight was no better.

Ryan is now 27 and lives with his partner and his son. It has come right for him. It became clear that he is clever and could achieve like other children. He is now a teaching assistant in a school for children with special needs and he loves it. Because of his challenges, he understands what is happening to some of the other children. I can remember the time when he wouldn't get into a car or go for a meal. Now he takes his son for a meal and to the football. He is bright and it has come right for him. It has been a team effort. We needed the support. I feel very proud. He lives in a nearby town, so we can meet easily. The main thing is what he has become. It has all happened right for him. I wish someone would have told me years ago it would end like this. I've always wanted an opportunity to say "thank you" to Family Fund.

Chapter 3

'A Coming Of Age', 1996–2023

A new charity is born

If 1973 to 1996 was about establishing Family Fund's independence and credibility, the years following 1996 have been characterised by growth, growing confidence and a period of extraordinary innovation. There is no doubt that the robust structure that had been put in place, the determination by the Joseph Rowntree Foundation to make its own decisions about eligibility, and the link with the University of York to record and interrogate data contributed greatly to ensuring 21 years of growing service to families. But with the 21st birthday, the Trustees decided that now was the time to cut free, establish Family Fund as a separate charity, and sever links with the very successful partnership they had had with Joseph Rowntree.

A paper to the JRF board, on the 21st birthday of Family Fund, recorded that expenditure had now increased to £16 million and dwarfed the Foundation itself; even if the Research and Development activities and housing operations were combined. There was no appetite for reconstituting Family Fund as a government agency but a feeling that it needed to be separated in some way from its parent. In a paper to the Board, Richard Best, the Director, proposed two potential ways forward. The first was a new trust separated from JRF and operating as an autonomous charity. The second, if this was seen as too disruptive, was to stay within the confines of JRF but with new reporting lines. It would involve expanding the Family Fund Management Board which would assume greater responsibility for the affairs of the organisation. Whichever of these two options was chosen Best argued that greater independence was needed, 'in recognition that it has, indeed, Come of Age'.

In 1996 the 'Family Fund Trust for families with severely disabled children' became an independent charity. The assets were transferred from JRF and the new charity was launched on Monday 22nd April by Gerald Malone, Minister of State at the Department of Health. The first meeting of the new Trustee Board took place the following day with terms establishing no fewer than three meetings a year, plus an AGM. Sir Peter Barclay, previously a trustee of JRF, agreed to chair for a year and declared that 'the great thing is that the Family Fund Trust is here to stay'. At the same time and with independence, the Department of Health decided to introduce a cash limit on its future grant-aid to Family Fund.

Just two years later, the nature of the funding changed, with income now coming from the national governments in England, Northern Ireland, Scotland and Wales. This guaranteed that support could continue to be delivered across the whole of the UK and made Family Fund one of the few publicly funded bodies to do this. It was essential that Family Fund responded to the growing devolution debate which resulted in the *1998 Scotland Act*, *Northern Ireland Act* and *Government of Wales Act*. It followed on from voters choosing, the previous year, to create a Scottish Parliament and a National Assembly for Wales. Devolution was also a key element of the Belfast (Good Friday) Agreement in 1998, equally supported by a referendum. Establishing new relationships in Scotland, Northern Ireland and Wales resulted in a closer understanding of the way needs differed in the four nations and allowed Family Fund to forge contacts with the governments as they separately evolved policies for families. Family Fund developed new measures of performance, accountability and transparency. It developed a network of visiting Advisers and Country Co-ordinators in England, Northern Ireland, Scotland and Wales, and concentrated on improving technical capabilities with a new IT system. By 1998 there were 12 regional co-ordinators and 190 visitors. Leaflets were produced in Welsh, Bengali, Chinese, Hindi, Gujarati,

Punjabi and Urdu. There was a new team of customer care staff to handle telephone enquiries and the range of support offered was extended to include, amongst other things, holidays overseas and housing adaptations.

Definitions of eligibility

What also characterised the early years of the 21st Century was a gradual refinement of those families who could be eligible to apply. It had already been necessary to introduce a level of means testing, based on family income, and this level was periodically reviewed. Family Fund had been greatly assisted by the social model of disability, which had moved assessment from what was often referred to as the straightjacket of a narrow medical definition of a particular condition, to a model where a child must have additional complex needs or a life-threatening illness. The child's additional needs must affect the family's choices and opportunity to enjoy an ordinary life and the degree of planning and support required to meet these needs must be greater than that usually required. The child must also require a high level of support in some of the areas such as the physical environment, education, communication, access to social activities, personal care and supervision. Finally, the child's condition must be long term or life limiting.

Eligibility was then further defined by the upper age limit that Family Fund supported at the time and entitlement to the appropriate benefits which would change over time. Of course, the applicants needed current legal residence in the UK; living in England, Wales, Scotland or Northern Ireland for at least the previous six months. The aim was to produce a flexible set of criteria, encouraging rather than deterring possible applicants.

From grant making to Making Voices Heard

With independence came a growing confidence and a determination by Family Fund to extend the work it did beyond the vital task of distributing grants to families. An early example of this was Family Fund's amalgamation with the 'Homes Fit for Children' campaign. It is a good instance of the way in which Family Fund's knowledge of what families faced – because of their direct contact with them – led to an awareness of larger scale and shared issues. It was realised that the-then present system of Disabled Facilities Grants, first introduced in 1996, to help with, for example, widening doors, converting bathrooms or providing a heating system, left many parents of disabled children with unrealistically large sums to pay toward the cost of essential adaptations to their homes. As a result, many decided not to go ahead and lost out on the benefits of successful adaptations. The Trust decided to join the Homes Fit for Children campaign, echoing Lloyd George's

'Homes Fit for Heroes', introduced at the end of the First World War. Together with RADAR (the Royal Association for Disability and Rehabilitation), the Association of Directors of Social Services, and the Council for Disabled Children, they campaigned for the grant system to make realistic allowances for family spending, especially on housing cost. Not only is it an example of an emerging pattern of picking up on national issues, but of Family Fund's confidence to stand with others for social and economic change. Chapter 4 of the book will deal specifically with both this and the projects that Family Fund has successfully developed since it became an independent charity.

By 2000 the-then Chief Executive Roger Mattingly had retired to be replaced by Marion Lowe and as part of the 30th anniversary – described by the Chair in his introduction as "still the same at 30, but better" – Family Fund embarked upon a new development which would have profound implications right the way through to the present day. Before this, Family Fund had regarded computers primarily as an educational tool for children and therefore the responsibility of the education authorities. But a new scheme, known as the Golden Freeway Project, was to change that. It was started as an attempt to reduce social isolation, by providing each family in the north of England who had a boy with Duchenne muscular dystrophy with a personal computer, email and internet connection – 74 out of 80 families from Cumbria, Durham, Northumberland, Teesside and Tyne and Wear with a child diagnosed before January 2000 had a computer installed. The aim was to encourage independence and self-esteem and reduce isolation.

Family Fund were quickly convinced of the value of this initiative. From February 2003 they began considering requests from families for computer equipment and in the last two months of that financial year made grants averaging £700 to families for computer equipment. As the Annual Report of that year noted, Family Fund had joined the 21st Century and feedback from the first 100 families who received such a grant was positive. In conjunction with this initiative, Family Fund broadened its website, encouraging families to use it as a source of information and as a way of encouraging them to apply. The 21st Century really had arrived!

The commitment of Family Fund has always been to the totality of communities that the four UK nations served. One theme in the early years of the 21st Century, particularly between 2003 and 2004, was the growing awareness that many groups including black and minority ethnic communities face additional challenges in gaining the help they need. Family Fund calculated that about 15% of all families helped were from black and minority ethnic communities and work was done to develop an improved service, including easy access to interpreters to increase face-to-face contact and produce more written material in appropriate languages. As part of an initiative to reach black and minority ethnic communities, Family Fund hosted an event with Trevor Phillips, then Chair of the Commission for Racial Equality. The importance of this work to reach communities has remained a constant theme for Family Fund and later discussion about the way information about grant recipients has become fine-tuned indicates Family Fund's determination to reach all who might need support.

By 2005/6 Family Fund had 150 advisors (the role previously designated as 'visitors'; see Chapter 6 for more information on staff roles) and continued modernising with the introduction of pre-payment cards, which families could receive instead of a cash grant and then use to buy household goods from a major high street retailer, ensuring that families had the same opportunities as other families to purchase items of their own choice. Additionally, this new method of awarding grants allowed Family Fund to receive a rebate on the money spent which was then returned to grant funds to help Family Fund award grants to even more families. It was part of an overall shift in terms of how Family Fund could extend its support, meet its obligations to funders and ensure choice and control to parents and carers. This approach marked another significant development which was to become part of Family Fund's relentless quest to make the money it received go further, and to raise further funding to support its charitable purpose. Working with retailers and suppliers allowed for favourable terms to be negotiated for other items, such as for white goods and beds. When Family Fund Trading was established, Family Fund was also looking at how it might be possible to negotiate other discounts for beneficiaries and how support could be extended. Similarly, as we shall see from fallout from Farepak (below), Family Fund was starting to develop innovative commercial partnerships to the benefit of its families. Family Fund was moving towards new commercial ventures.

Farepak

In 2006 Family Fund faced a new challenge, not of its own making. Farepak, a Christmas savings club and a subsidiary of the European Home Retail group, was plunged into administration. It had approximately 150,000 customers who chose Christmas hampers and vouchers in advance and then made regular payments, so that they could, for example, have toys and presents for children at Christmas. The total lost by Christmas savers was reckoned to be in the region of £42m and Family Fund first became aware when they were contacted by affected families.

Derek Walpole, Family Fund's deputy CEO at the time, was contacted by Sir Ian McCartney, then Minister of State for Trade, to see if Family Fund could help in any way as many families affected were those whom the charity would support. A combination of 30 years of distributing grants and the background of workable relationships with the four UK governments made Family Fund a natural first choice, and Family Fund had a track record of helping out in the face of national tragedy. The aspiration was to find some way of compensating affected families by ensuring that they had vouchers which could be used in time for Christmas. Together with the Department of Trade and Industry and Family Fund, the Farepak Response Fund was quickly launched, as an independent company with charitable staff, serviced by Family Fund's staff. It succeeded in collecting about £8 million from various corporate donors, including financial services companies and retailers. Between October and December 2006, with Family Fund candles burning into the night, the families affected were linked to their accounts and subsequent losses and lists submitted to the Park Group who, in turn, distributed vouchers free of charge to the families. About 5,000 families in receipt of Fund grants were also Farepak customers.

There is no doubt that this was a major achievement for Family Fund, executed in addition to the daily demands of grant distribution and demonstrating that the skills and experience which Family Fund had acquired could be turned to new directions. Derek Walpole, in turn, became Chairman of the newly created Christmas Pre-Payments Authority. This role also saw closer working with Ed Balls, then Secretary of State at the Department of Children, Schools and Families and even extended to a friendly football match at a school outside Wakefield as the result of the contact they had developed during the Farepak failure!

Farepak had demonstrated the growing possibility of Family Fund sub-contracting work for other organisations and the importance of raising funds to support the increasing needs of families who were reaching out for support. In 2009, with the recent appointment of a new Commercial Director, Cheryl Ward, Family Fund set up a website, called Family Fund Extra (FFE) that allowed families of disabled and seriously ill children to access discounts from retailers for products such as electrical items, holidays and household goods. FFE was also an affiliate site where those buying online could shop through the site, generating income for the charity. It was innovative and engaging but ahead of its time in offering a round up for charity donations via checkout whilst operating as an affiliate income site. Sadly, however, the level of marketing spend and promotion of the website was unable to reach a critical mass of customers and as time passed it was not able to compete with some other websites which later moved to allow income from affiliates to be paid straight to customers rather than to an organisation like Family Fund, and the site was closed.

Family Fund Trading

The Executive team of Family Fund were undaunted. By now they had accumulated years of experience grant-making and managing a supplier base. The goal of securing further income for the charity remained imperative. In 2012 the Welfare Reform Act was passed, making changes to the discretionary Social Fund to occur after April 2013. Responsibility for providing financial support in the form of grants and loans was devolved, while funding was made available to local authorities in England and to the devolved Administrations to provide such assistance as their areas saw fit. As part of the devolution of the Social Fund, Family Fund was invited to support the Department of Work and Pensions on a roadshow, visiting local authorities in order to demonstrate how the charity provided financial grant support with a set budget of grant funding. The roadshows highlighted the significant burden that many local authorities were feeling in taking on this responsibility. After learning more about the challenges and concerns that local authorities had in undertaking the devolution of the Social Fund, Family Fund saw a new opportunity.

"If ever there was a time to make a difference and grow our income it is now," Cheryl said.

Family Fund Trading was reborn. The company established to allow consumers to shop online as Family Fund Extra was re-purposed as Family Fund Trading to support local authorities in the practical delivery of welfare funding on the ground. Family Fund Trading was and remains a wholly owned trading subsidiary of the charity, focused on commercial and financial growth. The aim of the subsidiary was to generate profit which could be gifted as a donation to Family Fund, to help sustain and develop the work of the charity, particularly over and above the award of grants. With backing from the Board of Trustees and within a nine month period, a small team, initially four and later extending to six, had set up a business and had secured contracts with a number of local authorities providing fulfilment for their grant-making services, to ensure that their beneficiaries received the help they needed.

From its origins in 1973 Family Fund has been focused on ensuring that the maximum income was available to meet the needs of families. Today, Family Fund Trading (FFT) – or Family Fund Business Services (FFBS) as it became (see below) – still delivers a service, supporting not only local authorities but housing associations, national governments and other charities. The aim has always been twofold – to help other organisations stretch their funding further, but also to help generate income which is gifted as a donation to Family Fund, to support the sustainability of the charity, and its work supporting families with disabled and seriously ill children.

To bring this account of Family Fund's history up to the present day, by 2013 FFT was claiming two principal activities – offering services to other organisations, such as payroll and accountancy and also fulfilment to other grant-making organisations. In the same year, FFT – in partnership with Northgate – won a contract with the Welsh government to deliver the Wales Discretionary Assistance Fund. This success grew with FFT securing a further 27 contracts with local authorities, delivering services and generating income for the charity. The Partnership with Northgate (now NEC) delivering the Wales Discretionary Assistance Fund was renewed in 2017 and remains in place in 2023. In 2017, Family Fund Trading was rebranded as Family Fund Business Services (FFBS), to better reflect the services offered. Following this, between 2018 and 2019 FFBS gained new contracts with charities, housing associations and was successful in becoming the delivery partner of the BBC Children in Need Emergency Essentials Grant Scheme which was tendered in 2018. By 2022, FFBS employed 20 staff; cumulatively, since 2013, over £9m has been gifted to the charity from FFBS profits.

In a lot of instances this additional source of income to Family Fund has not only assisted with sustainability but helps the charity to deliver other functions such as research, technological development, and support with fundraising for the charity and matched funding to support other charitable schemes. Some will be outlined below and serve to illustrate how far Family Fund has come in its ability to reach families and their children.

A possible credit union

If we return to 2008, the year in which Family Fund Trading was set up, and the growth of the Charity's core activities, Family Fund also considered the feasibility of setting up a Family Fund credit union.

Research carried out by the University of York Social Policy Research Unit and published in an editorial in the *British Medical Journal* of November 2006 revealed that 55% of families with a disabled child lived in, or on the margins of, poverty. Calling upon their links with Family Fund, the study further revealed that of families registered with Family Fund, around 52% lived in social housing while the same proportion were lone parents. Thinking to develop a Family Fund credit union, the Charity argued that it could be particularly valuable to low- and middle-income families that did not reach the eligibility for grants from Family Fund but might benefit from additional financial support, without extortionate interest charges. Farepak had also demonstrated that putting money aside through a savings club that subsequently goes bust, could leave families in an even more precarious position.

Furthermore, many of the families that applied to Family Fund had heavy debts, whether these were to catalogues, childcare Tax Credit overpayments, or clubs. A credit union would therefore be beneficial both for savings, whether regular or occasional, and also for loans towards major family expenditure such as holidays, white goods or clothing. The feasibility study, conducted by the Association of British Credit Unions Limited, concluded that a credit union, for this target group was a feasible proposition, with the potential for delivering significant economic and social benefits, provided that there was a considerable cash investment at the outset. It would be member-owned, the criteria would be for families where there were children or young people under 16 with a severe disability, UK residency, savings of less than £18,000 and gross earned income of £23,000 in England, Northern Ireland and Scotland and £25,000 in Wales. It would be wider than just Fund beneficiaries and access would be through a Family Fund club. The Trustees finally decided not to go ahead with the scheme but, given the intelligence from Fund assessors, constantly testifying to the severe financial circumstances experienced by many of the families, the subsequent development of Family Fund was characterised by a range of initiatives aimed at addressing poverty, the avoidance of debt and the management of family finance.

From influence to action

The years following 2008, up to and including the onset of coronavirus, have seen an exponential growth in activities sitting alongside the core activity of making grants to families. Derek Walpole was followed as CEO in 2012 by Cheryl Ward, who, since 2008, had been the Commercial Director, and under her leadership Family Fund has demonstrated that its unrivalled knowledge of what life is like for the families of disabled children can lead to a wide range of support which goes beyond one-off grants. A separate section on campaigning and Family Fund initiatives is included later. The remainder of this chapter brings Family Fund's story up to date, including the huge challenges faced during the pandemic.

In 2010, Steve Jobs introduced the iPad at an Apple Press event and Family Fund were quick to realise the potential of this new tool to increase communication for some children.

> Paula, aged two, was born with a rare genetic condition which affects mobility and speech and causes developmental delay. Following a recommendation from her Portage worker, Family Fund helped with an iPad to aid her understanding of cause and effect as well as helping develop motor, speech, language and social skills.

The same year, 2011, saw the launch of 'Siblings Matter Too' and in Scotland the launch of the 'Take A Break' scheme, both schemes developed and delivered from the understanding of what families needed. Both of these are explored further when we come to look at the influence of Family Fund and its projects. Family Fund were also instrumental, that same year, in assisting the UK's leading cancer charity for children and young people, CLIC Sargent, in a research report on '*Counting the Costs of Cancer*'. Vital information on families with children who had been diagnosed with cancer was provided by Family Fund from their extensive database.

It is entirely appropriate that a charity like Family Fund, distributing government money, should be subject to periodic review and in 2013, a review conducted by the Moorhouse Consortium took place on behalf of the Department for Education. This followed on from the Korda and Co independent review in 1985 mentioned earlier, plus another review in 1988 which according to the Board minutes found Family Fund

> *'both efficient and cost effective... in distributing small grants on a nationwide basis'.*

Similarly, in 1999, a technical survey of the effectiveness of and continuing need for Family Fund, looking specifically at internal systems, asserted that with ninety pence in every pound directly allocated to grants,

> *'an over-riding observation of the Trust's philosophy and purpose is one of being established ahead of its time'.*

The Moorhouse Consortium review, however, was by far the most detailed. It contains some useful demographic information, listing numbers of disabled children across the four UK countries, the significantly higher costs of caring for a disabled child (three times higher than for non-disabled children) and the kinds of disabilities affecting children supported by Family Fund. The most numerous in 2011–12 were children on the autistic spectrum, followed by those with learning disabilities and hearing and communication challenges.

It looked both at some of the other initiatives launched by Family Fund and at Family Fund Trading. Its conclusions were firstly that Family Fund was

'run as a business with a charity angle'

and that, when compared with other models, it was well placed to carry on

'its unique role – representing the best package of low-risk efficiency and greatest impact on outcomes'.

Influencing and project activity generated by Family Fund has always sprung from the issues raised by families. In 2013, as Family Fund celebrated 40 years of operation, 'Tired All The Time' was launched recording the experience of over 2,000 parents and carers across the UK, bringing attention to the demands of caring for a child with disabilities and the impact on parents and carers, notably sleep deprivation. In order both to bring the work of Family Fund to a wider audience and to publicise this new project, the Chief Executive and Partnership Manager led presentations in all four of the UK parliamentary buildings. More of this will be discussed under influencing and projects. It was to lead to the launch of a pilot for the Tired Out sleep support hub in 2016 and, in the same year, a Sleep Pathway pilot project of workshops in Lincoln helping 57 families in collaboration with the Sleep Charity.

Again, in the 40th anniversary year and to reduce paper and increase efficiency, Family Fund launched a new Family Fund On-line account, with an initial registration of 30,000 families. It allowed them to apply, track progress and view communications after registering for an account, and it also speeded up the application process.

What also came to characterise the years following 2016 was a series of partnerships with other organisations. Between 2016/17 the Advice and Support Service was launched in partnership with Contact a Family, providing 1,493 families with additional support on issues such as access to benefits, condition-specific advice and signposting to other forms of support. The same year saw the start of Reboot UK with Good Things Foundation, Homeless Link and MIND to help improve families' digital skills. The explosion of computer technology and the increasing demands from children for devices such as iPads led to a need for training as well. As a result of Reboot UK, training to 349 families or young people who had received a digital device from Family Fund was provided via one-to-one training or group workshops.

This was followed in 2017/18 with Building Digital Confidence; training which helped increase the participants' knowledge and skill and highlighted the difference that training can make.

> "I didn't realise how much could be done on the iPad and how it can be restricted for children. The training was brilliant and really made me feel more confident with using it and not seem stupid with the questions and lack of knowledge that I had before starting. I am so pleased that this type of training is offered as, without it, I would have been really struggling."
>
> Course participant

Between 2019 and 2020, as part of Good Things Foundation and the J.P. Morgan Chase Foundation's Power Up programme, Family Fund delivered both on-line and in-person learning and resources to enable families and carers in Edinburgh and Glasgow to better manage their finances.

Lastly, in terms of partnerships, Family Fund began a pilot project in 2017–18 with the Motability Tenth Anniversary Trust, assisting with provision of car leases to families with children under the age of three with significant mobility support needs who, because of their age, are not eligible to receive the mobility component of the Disability Living Allowance. This pilot project was then followed in 2020–22 by another, with the scheme now funded by Motability the Charity and no longer as a pilot.

The income from Family Fund Business Services (FFBS) mentioned above has funded various areas of work within the charity, one notable area being fundraising which is now developing in the charity. The focus is on supporting families where statutory funding is not offered and is supported by the Trustees, following a period of time that focussed heavily on the development of FFBS. Examples of this fundraising success can be evidenced through links with the Garfield Weston Foundation, the Moondance Foundation, the Marian Elizabeth Trust, Flora's Fund, the Pears Foundation, Big Lottery and Good Things Foundation to name some of those supporting the projects developed from the voice of families with disabled or seriously ill children. Family Fund has come a long way from a sole reliance on government funding as the only source of support to families. Indeed, it is the charitable status of Family Fund that has made applications to trusts and foundations possible.

2020 – a year like no other

Covid 19, which started in China as 'pneumonia of an unknown cause', was first identified in December 2019. The disease has not only had profound effects on the UK but, for our purposes, particularly on the lives of families with disabled children. From March 2020 lockdown commenced: schools were closed, people were placed on furlough or were working from home, others lost their jobs or were put on short-hours working and any kind of social life as previously experienced just ceased to exist. It is scarcely possible to understand the profound implications this had for many but specifically for families and children with a disability or serious illness. For many families, already struggling to make ends meet, income was reduced, the vital lifeline of schooling stopped, to be replaced by home schooling. Hospital and medical appointments largely stopped; for many of the children, their medical conditions made them especially vulnerable to an illness scarcely understood.

Family Fund had to make a quick transition to home working but ensure that its office remained operational, supporting those families whose applications could only be received in paper form. With admirable foresight, research to evaluate the impact on families was initiated and operationally the IT department moved quickly to ensure staff could continue to work and make grants from home and support services could continue. The office remained open for a group of staff, whilst others worked at home and many became accustomed to a blended routine of working at home and in the office as restrictions lightened. Family Fund was very aware that, because of digital inequalities, it was necessary to maintain paper application forms for those not comfortable with information technology, while at the same time doing as much as possible remotely and in line with government guidance to avoid the spread of the virus. This meant rethinking many areas, including office working, assessment visits and the way in which support to the families could be provided as concerns of low stock levels of essential grant items started to emerge. There was an increase in applications from families who, acknowledging the change to their lives, sought support for outdoor play equipment and digital devices, and for families deprived of days out or breaks Family Fund fostered the idea of 'a break at home'.

> "In a world where every day can be hard, Family Fund provide the small things which make a massive difference."
> A carer

We will look later at Family Fund's research data but there is little doubt that the effects on the mental and physical health of families with disabled children has been considerable. The true level of stress and disruption to family life may never be fully understood.

As a result of sharing with funders the impact on families and as a result of the pandemic, the UK Governments stepped forward to support the charity to meet the increasing needs of families. On top of the £27.3 million already committed for 2020/21 in England the Department for Education secured an extra £10 million from the Department for Digital, Culture, Media and Sport (part of a package of funding to enable organisations to continue their work to support people and communities in need during the Covid-19 pandemic) and then granted a further £3.5m the following January. Family Fund calculated that they were able to support an additional 20,000 families and a total of 90,791 grants in England were awarded – an increase of 28,537 on the previous year. In Scotland the core grant of £2.97m was supplemented by £880,000 both for grants to families and for the very successful 'Take A Break' scheme. A total of 8,468 grants were provided to Scottish families as a result. In Northern Ireland the Department of Health's agreed grant of £1.57m was supplemented by an additional £480,000, enabling 5,426 grants (a 32% increase on the previous year). Lastly, in Wales the grant funding of £360,000 was topped up by a further £158,000 and an increase of 32% on the previous year's grants. Despite all the constraints of the pandemic, Family Fund continued to gather the voices of families and five waves of on-line surveys in 2020/21 resulted in contact with 13,284 families, reaching 17,366 disabled children across the UK.

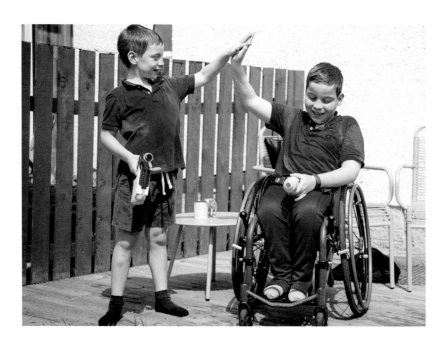

The results revealed that

- 96% of families reported that the health and wellbeing of their seriously ill and disabled children had been negatively affected

- behaviour and mental health were most negatively affected

- two thirds said support from healthcare services had declined

- three quarters said that overall their financial situation had worsened.

Clearly, Family Fund was far from unique in having to deal with an unprecedented and unforeseen global pandemic. But the nimbleness with which staff started to work in new and untried ways, the success in achieving extra funding (plus the realisation from the four UK governments that any extra investment would be well spent) and the willingness, as always, to listen to the needs of families, again demonstrated Lord Seebohm's words that Family Fund has been 'a resounding success'.

But it was not just the nimbleness in responding to extra demand that was appreciated by families, but also the change in the requests themselves. Family Fund saw an increase in referrals for digital devices – for home schooling and entertainment – and in grants for outdoor play and exercise equipment. Independent research from the NatCen Social Research (Britain's largest independent social research organisation) positively evaluated the contribution Family Fund had made during the pandemic.

We cannot conclude this chapter without recording a significant corporate partnership that Family Fund made during this period and in the midst of the pandemic. In another move forward the Trustees agreed a three-year partnership with McCain Foods, who pledged that, by 2023 they would have donated £1 million to help Family Fund reach their aim of providing 150,000 grants and services to families; they would also raise awareness of Family Fund. The funding was used to bring together families at meal times with grants for cookers, dining room tables and chairs and other support which enables families to come together and enjoy the little moments and importance of family time. The launch of the partnership was accompanied by television adverts, concentrating on some of the children and young people Family Fund supports. Not only did this represent a significant commercial partnership but it has led to a wider public awareness of the work Family Fund does. With the support of the McCain partnership Family Fund has been the focus of podcasts starring celebrities with lived experience of bringing up children with complex needs. Once more, Family Fund demonstrated its willingness to extend new pathways which would increase the help and support available to families and disabled children.

The 2000s – Mandy and Liam

I first applied to Family Fund when Liam was five. It was very much on the recommendation of other families. To be honest, I didn't know anything about Family Fund. I had a lovely assessment from a visitor who still works for Family Fund. Following this home visit, the assessor told me what might be available for Liam and since then we have had holidays, a new tumble dryer, clothing and other things. Frankly, it was a godsend. Liam has a younger sister, Megan. He has multi-disabilities – amongst other things, mild cerebral palsy, epilepsy, ADHD, autism, moderate learning difficulties and he suffers from severe anxiety.

It's been an evolving journey. He was a premature baby – 3lbs from the off. He is now 31 and back living with us. He was in assisted accommodation, but he was too anxious (not helped by the restrictions around the pandemic) and he has now moved back home. We're a resilient family and after the first grant we re-applied in subsequent years. Normally, it was a holiday grant because when you're on holiday you're just a family and you are away from intrusive professionals. Your life is not your own if you have a disabled child. You're always having to respond to multi-disciplinary teams. On holiday you can get away from all of this. With a disabled child you lose your identity. I became 'Liam's mum'. When you go away you do so as a family. And we usually went with my mum as well.

Liam has developed a love of music. He applied to Family Fund for an acoustic and an electric guitar. It felt like 'guilt-free shopping'. Obviously, the other things from Family Fund were very helpful, but this felt like the guitars were gifted to him. He's still got his guitars although now he spends more time taking them to pieces than playing them.

At one stage we had some adaptations to the house, through a Disabled Facilities grant and, again, Family Fund were helpful. They helped with furniture and carpets. They've just been there at the right time.

Liam's sister Megan has always been very resilient. She has always been supportive and has never shown any resentment. Now she has two children of her own.

As far as other services are concerned, I have always been self-sufficient and have known what else was available. Today we live in a very different world from when Liam was small, and signposting is very important. Sometimes families find it very difficult and, rather than money, they need someone to talk to – to give advice. Disability is an evolving thing. Liam's needs today are very different from when he was a 12-year-old. The transition to adult services is also very difficult and many families miss out on available services but, as young adults, they are entitled to a life of their own and the required support should always be available.

As a carer it is easy to become exhausted. Disability changes you. I refuse to let it define me but the impact is huge, not just for me as a parent but for the family as a whole. I work for Family Fund as do my daughter and sister – it feels right to be able to 'give something back'. I can see that Family Fund has become a huge support system which is no longer just about grants. It is the 'go-to' place for disability. It's a large organisation today, more than a grant provider – more a service provider. And it's not just about ticking boxes. This is their lives; every story is different and we respect that. I'm proud to tell people what I do. We're the best kept secret and should be part of the induction of every social worker.

Mandy Murphy, *Eligibility and Quality Assurance Supervisor, Family Fund*

Chapter 4

An Insightful Friend: Projects, campaigns and interns

It was evident from day one that the Family Fund would not just be a grant-giving body, but would want to influence policy and, in some circumstances, work with others to campaign for change. It will be recalled how there was initial discussion over the issue of criteria, the dropping of the term 'severely congenitally disabled', and the gradual movement towards what would now be defined as a social model of disability that focuses more on the barriers that are placed by society rather than on any impairment or difference. What was important was the extent to which a child was disadvantaged. Indeed, in the very first meeting with representatives of the DHSS, Family Fund argued that there must be flexibility of interpretation and any guidelines should be couched in as general terms as possible, in order to avert criticism. In this context, starting off as part of the Joseph Rowntree Trust was extremely helpful. Although the Foundation had not directly run services, their widespread experience of social policy was extremely valuable. They had regularly campaigned, and it meant Family Fund had easy access to those levers for which JRT had become known. Once the issue of *criteria* for receiving a grant had settled down in the first few years and severity became more important than cause, the issue to which Family Fund kept returning – threaded through the debate like the name of a seaside town throughout a stick of rock – was that of *eligibility* in terms of the age of children Family Fund could help.

The age of the child

When Family Fund was established, it was clearly understood that the charity was making grants to the families of children even though an age limit was not mentioned. It was quickly determined that 16 was to be the cut-off point, as this was the age at which young people became eligible for Supplementary Benefit. In the early days, people of all ages asked for help, including families caring for adults with a learning disability in their 30s or 40s, as well as those looking after elderly relatives. While discussion as to whether 16 was too early as a cut-off point started fairly early in the history of the board, Family Fund, in conjunction with the Social Policy Research Unit of York University published (and regularly updated) a booklet called '*After Age 16 – What Next?*' (1984). It provided information on benefits, allowances and grants for young people over the age of 16, when they were no longer eligible for Family Fund's support. They also issued advice about education and staying on at school after 16, open learning, youth training schemes and supported employment. It was also supplemented by information on useful organisations that could offer support.

Regularly, the Executive and Trustees discussed what seemed like an increasingly arbitrary cut-off point at 16 years old and began arguing for an extension to at least 18. In the 2006/7 Annual Report and under the heading of 'Not So Sweet 16' is a quote from a government review on the transition to adulthood as being vital to young people's independence and a report on a mother and her son who had Asperger's syndrome and was partially deaf. Through Family Fund the son was provided with a computer, a year's free internet access and a holiday grant which provided a long weekend break in Bath. But, with the advent of the son's 16th birthday no more help was available.

> "The government doesn't seem to realise that, when our kids hit 16, they need our help even more. They are all struggling while their friends are flying."
> Mother

In 2008–9, Family Fund first secured funding from the Department for Education in England to help 16- and 17-year-olds. Building on this and ever resourceful, in 2018 Family Fund launched a new grant scheme that began to address the long-held ambition to do more to help young people aged 18 and over, who face a challenging and difficult time as they transition into adult services. During the summer of 2018 Family Fund conducted focus groups with young people to find out what help they felt was needed and how Family Fund could achieve those outcomes. The respondents stated that they needed support with education and employment, as well as help to have fun, build friendships and improve their wellbeing. The result of this consultation was 'Your Opportunity', a scheme providing grants to help some of the challenges faced including help with social and leisure opportunities, education and employment. Your Opportunity was initially funded by the Edward Gostling Foundation and designated funding from Family Fund. The scheme began providing grants in January 2019 and was soon also supported by Pears Foundation in conjunction with the Edward Gostling Foundation who have extended their funding commitment.

Two major factors have assisted Family Fund in their influencing and project work, allowing them to 'speak truth to power', and to do this with an authoritative voice. The first of these is the tens of thousands of applications they receive every year, the direct contact with parents and carers and a first-hand account of what it is they need for their children. The staff and assessors hear the family stories, get close to their lives and offer support in a range of ways. The second is an unrivalled database, which provides epidemiological, educational, financial, housing and social information about the families who are supported. As we shall see below, projects which have extended Family Fund's work beyond the distribution of grants have sprung directly from the information provided by parents and carers. A further development, over the fifty years, is an increasing focus on being an 'insightful friend', to make the case for change with governments and policy makers alike but only speaking with the voice of parents and carers. Since funding has never been secure long term and Family Fund is competing with many more demands on government income, the Charity has been relentless in keeping the needs of families with disabled children on the agendas of the governments of Scotland, Wales, Northern Ireland and England directly and through collaborations and coalitions, such as

- the Disabled Childrens Partnership – a coalition of more than 100 organisations who campaign for improved health and social care for disabled children, young people and their families (England)

- the Scottish Government's Disabled Children's and Young People's Advisory Group

- Northern Ireland's Children with Disabilities Strategic Alliance, which seeks to ensure that policy impacting on the lives of disabled children and young people is informed by their needs and circumstances.

Family income for grant recipients

One of the most fundamental issues which has preoccupied Family Fund since its inception has been the average income levels of parents and carers. The 2005/6 Annual Report recorded that 90% of families helped by Family Fund had an income from employment below the-then UK average of £23k a year and that nearly a third were living in poverty. Sometimes, as we shall see, campaigning has been done alone, but with growing credibility, Family Fund was encouraged to be part of lobbying consortia.

In the early days of Family Fund, responding to financial and other pressures on families was very much based on informing carers of available services. So, in 1994, 'Taking Care' was published by the Joseph Rowntree Foundation, based on the partnership with York University and involving researchers, practitioners and families. As well as allowing families to talk about their experiences, it also made a number of important statements to service providers, and outlined ways in which resources could be used imaginatively, to care for their disabled sons and daughters. Early focuses for Family Fund were on the inadequacy of benefits, the constant pressure to avoid debt and issues such as the inadequacy of much housing. In 1997 Family Fund was involved in representation to government in its review on charity taxation. The fact that eligibility for Family Fund inevitably meant that families were on low incomes, allowed assessors to experience, daily, the struggles over finance that carers faced. This is why so much of Family Fund's influencing – across all four nations – has been aimed at attempting to increase financial support for families.

One of the most successful collaborative pieces of research, linked to family income, was that undertaken by the Family Fund and 'Contact a Family' in Wales. It was undertaken in 2012 and aimed to investigate the relationship between families with disabled children in Wales and child poverty. This was one of those studies that was able to draw upon Family Fund's unrivalled database, linking up postcodes for grant recipients with the Welsh Index of Multiple Deprivation (WIMD).

The study concluded that the highest concentration of families with disabled children was to be found in the most deprived WIMD areas of Wales. It briefly examined income, health, education, community safety, housing, the physical environment and geographical access to services, concluding that Family Fund provided vital support to families with disabled children living in the most deprived areas of Wales and calling on the Welsh government to offer more support.

Widening the scope of influence: an insightful friend

The success of this initiative has led to a range of partnerships with other organisations. Income levels have figured largely and included links with the Disabled Children's Partnership (of which Family Fund is a member), End Child Poverty and 'Keep the Lifeline', a campaign which was coordinated by the Joseph Rowntree Foundation and the Trussell Trust in 2021, calling on the UK government not to cut the lifeline of the Covid-related uplift of £20 a week in Universal Credit and Working Tax Credit.

What has become increasingly evident is that the foundation of a strong database and thousands of parent and carers' voices has strengthened the determination of Family Fund to widen those ways in which they might act as an insightful friend. The 2016/17 Annual Report announced a plan to develop a public affairs and research team, as part of a new strategy to increase internal research and outcome reporting. Alongside the collaborative research and campaigns undertaken with other organisations, Family Fund wanted to become more active at responding to formal policy consultations, sharing research and engaging with government departments across the four UK nations.

For example, in 2021/22 Family Fund responded to nine consultations across the four nations. This included the Treasury Committee's 'An Equal Recovery' inquiry which examined different forms of inequality that had been exacerbated by the pandemic. Family Fund's response to this highlighted the disproportionately negative impact the pandemic had had on disabled people, minority ethnic families and women.

In Scotland, Family Fund responded firstly to the Scottish government's *'Ending the Need for Food Banks: A draft national plan'* (2021) by proposing that food insecurity could be reduced by providing long-term funding for community groups. Secondly, Family Fund responded to the consultation on *'Winter Heating Benefits: Low income winter heating assistance'*, which proposed to replace the Cold Weather Payment with a new benefit based solely on receipt of a low income benefit.

In Northern Ireland, Family Fund assisted with the Department of Education's consultation on the *Children and Young People Strategy. Initial 3-year Delivery Plan 2021–2024* and, separately, led a focus group with parents and carers alongside the Department for Communities to develop a strategy to tackle inequalities and obstacles affecting everyday life. In these, as with other initiatives, Family Fund has become adept, where helpful, at holding family focus group sessions, contributing to collective campaign work, sharing research with governments and engaging with government departments by accessing data which support policy work.

Finally, two more areas need highlighting, as examples of the way Family Fund's influence has spread far beyond the huge contribution made by grant giving alone. The introduction of Family Polls and projects will be considered in more detail elsewhere in the book, but deserves noting as part of Family Fund's influencing armoury.

The introduction of Family Polls, deriving from information held on the database, has permitted Family Fund to draw up an accurate profile of the families who apply for grants. From a sample that is nationally representative of the families on low incomes raising children with disabilities, researchers can, for example, examine the average amount of care needed for a disabled child, numbers in the household in employment, use of specialist equipment and, since 2019, factors affecting the families as a direct or indirect consequence of Covid. All of this is not only useful in terms of influencing to improve services but by reporting to the four UK governments how increased funding could be used by children and their families. The kind of profile information produced will be considered elsewhere.

The last examples of influencing, by being an insightful friend, lie in the way Family Fund has used its reach and knowledge not only to develop projects addressing issues raised by parents, carers and staff, but also to provide a model of what might be developed elsewhere. So 'Siblings Matter Too', 'Tired All The Time' and the Scottish 'Take A Break' scheme – all discussed below – give three examples where the identification of real challenges for parents and carers have been transformed into practical actions and solutions for children and their families.

I suspect few voluntary organisations can confidently outline so much transformation and evolution over 50 years. Sir Keith Joseph, stepping cautiously between responding to the needs of families learning to cope with thalidomide and not wanting to propose a financial solution which would allow Distillers to withdraw financial help, could scarcely have imagined that

Family Fund would even exist 50 years later. He certainly would not have foreseen that in addition to maintaining support from all four UK governments, through a careful annual presentation of unmet need, Family Fund would also be campaigning for better services, making the case for increases in financial support for families and becoming a major player in the voluntary sector disability lobby influencing for change — and all achieved as a firm, well researched and insightful friend.

From influencing to direct action

In many ways it makes sense that a forward-thinking charity that has segued from providing grants to influencing as well might also wish to identify the gaps in services by developing its own project solutions. This has only been made possible by a combination of insight from families, a dedicated and knowledge-based team and additional income generated by Family Fund Business Services and, most recently, income raised by fundraising. Four examples: Tired All The Time, Take A Break, Sibling Matters Too and a range of initiatives to increase both digital skills and financial planning will help to demonstrate Family Fund's versatility.

Tired All The Time

Family Fund became increasingly aware of the challenges faced at night by parents and carers of children with disabilities. This could be because children needed turning during the night, or the administration of medical procedures, difficulties with sleep patterns and the complexity of establishing sleep routines or, for some children, the incomprehension of distinguishing night from day. In July 2013 Family Fund launched 'Tired All The Time', a report on sleep deprivation amongst families raising disabled children. Two thousand parents and carers were consulted and there was also a pilot project evaluated by the University of Hull.

The report was launched in the parliaments of all four nations between July and October 2013 and was followed up by a support hub for families to find help and information about sleep issues. This included information about bedtime routines, sensory influences, availability of sleep services in the area, sleep tips, research leads and what could be learnt from other families.

As one family, responding to the advice recorded:

> "Bedtime in our house is often filled with chasing our youngest around the house, trying to get his PJs on, and at some level trying to keep the bedroom routine calm. We are very firm when it comes to his bedtime, it's something that we both agreed on after our eldest daughter wouldn't sleep! Is it easy? Hell no. But it works!"
>
> Parent

When we come to look at the 'Take A Break' scheme, we will see other ways in which Family Fund has tried to address the considerable challenge some families face from lack of sleep over months and sometimes years.

Siblings Matter Too

While there is a growing literature and research on the challenges faced by young carers – many of whom share the responsibility of looking after disabled parents – there is less information on the role siblings play towards their brothers and sisters. Yet siblings – as Family Fund came to understand – face a unique set of challenges. Their sleep may be disturbed; it is sometimes difficult to get parental attention; there may be less opportunity for their own space and interests; they may experience bullying at school or be required to stick up for their brothers and sisters; and home life may be disrupted in hundreds of small ways. They are often overlooked, are not always identified by local authorities and schools, and few are supported by agencies such as the Children and Adolescent Mental Health Services. As one 17-year-old sibling said:

> "I think that being a sibling you get your ups and downs anyway... but just because there is the added bit of the disability sometimes you don't know what she is going to do or how she's going to take it or react, you have to be a bit more careful because it can be a bit of a rollercoaster, up and down."

Following research drawing on the experiences of siblings, parents, and carers, Family Fund wanted to do more: £100,000 of funding was secured from a private donor to acknowledge the contribution that siblings make to family life through a small grant scheme. This grant provided an opportunity for siblings themselves to receive something that made a difference to them. Further funding was later secured from a number of other donors and the Trustees also agreed to provide increased funding to recognise siblings from the charity's unrestricted income. The level of grant making increased from 150 grants given to siblings in 2013/14, to over 1,000 in 2019/20.

> "Emma was chuffed to bits and felt so appreciated. She not only cares for her brother but also me, as I suffer from depression, so life can be really hard for her. She is a member of a young carer's federation."
>
> Mother of Emma

Alongside these grants, Family Fund entered a research partnership with the University of Portsmouth and published a report in October 2015, both to examine the effectiveness of the grants and raise awareness of the issues more widely. Issues highlighted in the report ranged from elements of a typical sibling relationship, complications around the lack of time, and daily experiences including aggression, violence and emotional distress. Here was another example of Family Fund seeing a very real challenge to families and coming up with solutions which may not have removed those challenges but could help to alleviate them.

In the same way, Family Fund recognised the contribution that grandparents made to the lives of disabled and seriously ill children when it launched its report '*I Wish I Could Be Grandma*' at the House of Lords with the late Lord Brian Rix. The 2011–12 Annual Report, for example, records 1,128 families were supported with grants where the grandparents were the main carers.

Take A Break

Take A Break is a striking example of Family Fund's constant desire to develop the way it delivers support to families with a disabled child and help others to find practical solutions that can empower parents and retain choice and control. The scheme is one of two grant programmes funded by the Scottish government as part of the Health and Wellbeing programme, and has been developed and administered by Family Fund since it was first piloted in 2011–12. It provides grants to unpaid carers of disabled children and young people who have complex additional support needs or serious or life-threatening conditions. These grants allow carers to access a break from caring in a way of their choosing. As such it fits naturally into the provision of help to parents and other carers whose children might well be recipients of

Fund grants. Initially, between 2012–13, 1,300 families were helped, increasing to 1,600 the following year. As one recipient recorded:

> *"The holiday helps all of our mental health. It gives everyone a chance to breathe and relax. All the staff where we go know our son and it's like an extended family."*

The scheme was championed on the ground by Salena Begley MBE, Scotland's Family Fund Partner Engagement Manager. In 2021, the Take A Break scheme received 3,600 applications, 1,370 of which were from first time applicants; 97% of recipients reported that the break was beneficial, helping them to sustain their caring role and to be closer to other people, with improved wellbeing and a greater ability to deal with problems on their return. Furthermore, 24% felt that, as a result of the break, their disabled child was achieving more. In terms of age profile, the biggest groups were those with children aged 6–10 and 11–15 with popular grants being used for breaks away, days out, outdoor equipment and camping. The Scottish government had increased the scheme in 2020–21 to £1.5m. For Family Fund, it has been a natural extension of its work and for the people of Scotland it was another way of practically responding to the Tired All The Time campaign.

From 'Power Up' to iPad summer schools

This final section deals with a range of projects which not only demonstrate the creativity within Family Fund but also its ability to respond to the emerging needs of carers. They can be divided in three major ways:

- Firstly, by means of funding with income provided by Family Fund Trading or from grant making bodies, as Family Fund has become more adept at locking into funding from other grant making bodies.

- Secondly, in terms of the projects developed, ranging from computer and IT training to a combination of IT training and financial planning and schemes developed through other partnerships.

- Lastly, through developing spin-offs for families, some of which were inevitably more successful than others.

Family Fund quickly became aware that the explosion in digital technology created a requirement for families to become IT literate. It developed new approaches to engaging families in order to improve their digital skills and thereby increase confidence. It also developed a peer mentoring skill, a little like the medical model of 'see one, do one, teach one'. Family Fund in Scotland had a programme in conjunction with the Scottish government to develop digital confidence. For all of those who were recipients of Family Fund-purchased iPads, there was a series of iPad workshops on 'Getting Started', 'Make It Work for You' and (given the potential dangers of on-line access), 'Staying Safe'.

In 2020 and very much as a result of the Covid lockdown, Family Fund also began an iPad summer school, with help from its new partner, the Royal National Institute for Blind People. It was launched both as an opportunity for families to build on their creative digital skills and to have fun at the same time. In this way, virtual workshops have examined how to make a movie, by using iMovie, making songs using GarageBand and creating your own comic strips, using Clips. All the sessions were led by an Apple accredited trainer. In 2021, 81% of parents involved in the programme reported their child or young person's wellbeing had improved largely through increased confidence. As one family recorded:

> "Peter's attention is awful, he can't sit still, so I thought it would be good to have something for us to do. If he's on his iPad, he can focus easier. After talking with Family Fund, I realised that I could do the sessions with him, or on another tablet. That meant that if he didn't feel up to it, I could learn the skills during the session and then teach him later when he felt better."
>
> Parent

Given the 2020–21 research finding by Family Fund that half of the families surveyed had lost income since lockdown began, it also seemed logical to make a link between technology and financial advice and planning. Following a successful collaboration and grant through the Good Things Foundation, Power Up was developed which provided digital knowledge to empower families to improve their long-term financial health within the cities of Glasgow and Edinburgh. (Between 2021–22, 373 families were trained in digital skills in Scotland.) A smaller grant, again from the Good Things Foundation, also supported families who were in receipt of tax credits, to ensure that they were receiving the disabled child element of tax credits. This was more specific but fitted in with the general aim of ensuring that families both knew of financial opportunities and had the digital skills to maximise their income.

Reference was made earlier to Family Fund's growing awareness of fundraising as a way of extending its reach to families. Family Fund's approach to fundraising was unusual as it started with a trading subsidiary and then moved into the more typical fundraising approaches seen in the charity sector. Between 2017–18 Family Fund was successful in receiving £100,000 from the Garfield Weston Foundation to support families in Wales. There had been a shortfall in funding from the Welsh government and this grant helped in supplementing the number of awards that could be made by Family Fund. Similarly, following a meeting with a private donor Family Fund developed a grant scheme for the Marian Elizabeth Trust which provides a grant to support families caring for children and young adults with 'multiple, complex significant learning and physical support needs', living in Liverpool, the Wirral and the Midlands. A grant from Flora's Fund was given to support families with children affected by cystic fibrosis.

The last two examples of Fund creativity are centred upon assisting families, albeit at the margins, to improve the quality of their lives and, where possible, ease their financial situation. One example was the provision of dedicated travel insurance. With the growth in popularity of grants for holidays, families often found the insurance needed for some medical conditions made the grant difficult to accept. Support from a dedicated insurance scheme could make all the difference between a family having the opportunity to take an overseas break and them being unable to take up the grant offered.

Aware of the sheer time-pressures families faced, the charity launched a new Family Fund online account in July 2013, with 30,000 families quickly registering to use the service. Again, it represented a cost-efficient way of administering Family Fund and the use of technology to ease the grant process for many applicants. There is plenty of evidence to demonstrate not only that the pace of change within Family Fund has increased in recent years but that the organisation's willingness to innovate in response to families' demands has not diminished. Across the 50 years it is scarcely possible to grasp how far a system to provide financial support for families has opened itself to so many imaginative developments and spin-offs.

Supporting interns

Support from Family Fund has always extended to a wide group of recipients and, in the very early days, work placements were provided for female prisoners from Askham Grange, southwest of York. Work experience opportunities were extended to local schools and colleges and specifically to Appleby's School where students with a disability experienced working in the Charity. More recently, Family Fund has begun providing supported internships with the support of Blueberry Academy and is now entering into its second year and achieving great outcomes. One of these interns now works for Family Fund in a permanent role, the second has found paid employment elsewhere and the third is continuing with learning.

Building on this, and through the continued partnership with the Blueberry Academy, Family Fund took on two new supported interns and offered a work placement for a third. Through the internships they have not only provided work experience but also new skills and confidence which can be taken to new settings. Two of the interns, who took part in the scheme are in little doubt about its effectiveness.

> "I love working at Family Fund. I feel like I am doing something to help and change lives. At the end of the day I can think, 'Well I have done something good today'. I've learnt to be more confident with myself, being able to speak to other people I don't know."
>
> Family Fund/Blueberry Academy intern

Links with organisations like the Blueberry Academy are what Family Fund does well. Formed in 2007 and based in York, the Academy supports young people between the ages of 16 and 25 to progress into independence and employment. Their vision is very similar to that of Family Fund, aiming to provide equal life chances for young people with disabilities as they move into adulthood. The kind of sustainable paid employment that Family Fund has offered fits neatly into their overall mission. Alongside the projects and campaigns, it demonstrates the way Family Fund lives its values, taking young people to the next stage with employment and feelings of self-worth.

Isaac's Story

I adopted Isaac when he was 18 months old. I also adopted his older sister, Andraya, when she was two. It wasn't until I had Isaac for six months that he received his diagnosis. I had worked with special education needs children before so I suspected that Isaac wasn't developing as he should be, so I took Isaac to see a paediatrician who quickly realised what his condition was.

Isaac was diagnosed with Foetal Alcohol Spectrum Disorder (FASD). FASD is classed as organic brain damage which first occurs within the womb when the foetus is growing. If the birth mother drinks alcohol, then the foetus will absorb the alcohol and as a result the baby's stem cells will be damaged.

The condition affects Isaac's brain and how he sees the world. Now that Isaac is eight, he can become overwhelmed and aggressive easily and his behaviour is unpredictable and impulsive. On some occasions, we can predict that a meltdown is coming, but sometimes we haven't got a clue. Additionally, the part of Isaac's brain which is damaged means that he doesn't produce melatonin. As a result, he has a poor sleeping pattern and struggles to function when tired.

Isaac is outgoing, very bubbly, and easy to like. He loves playing Minecraft on his iPad and gardening. As a family, we enjoy the outdoors together.

Caring for Isaac is a full-time job. I had to give up work to look after him since his needs are so complex. We need to do everything for Isaac, from getting him dressed and fed. It's like having an eighteen-month year old in a seven-year old's body.

Family Fund are a life saver. If it wasn't for the grants that they provide, I probably would have had a breakdown. You don't realise how great the impact of the grants are until you receive one. I could never have afforded the grant items on my own.

We've received several grants over the years including outdoor play equipment, sensory items, a washing machine, and family breaks. The washing machine grant was especially a great help. Isaac used to love to sit in front of the washing machine and watch it go around. Also, due to

his brain damage, Isaac urinates a lot and can sometimes wet the bed so we often have a lot of washing to do. The grant from Family Fund allowed me to upgrade my washing machine from 5kg to 9kg.

In recent years, we have received family break grants. We go to the same Haven holiday park every year. Everybody there knows him and they give us the same caravan each time. When we arrive, Holly who works there, greets us which is lovely. The break offers us all a massive chance to recharge and feel relaxed after living at home and trying to manage schooling and meltdowns.

Family Fund has had a huge impact in the lives of Isaac and our family.

Chapter 5

The Laura Ashley Brigade – Staff and Signposting

Having in 1973 accepted the government's brief to assess and distribute funds to families, the Joseph Rowntree Foundation had to set up systems to make this possible. An early tussle centred upon whether the assessors should all be professional social workers. In his book on the Joseph Rowntree Foundation, Lewis Waddilove (Waddilove, 1983) recounts that considerable pressure was put on the Trustees to accept a view that decisions on grants should be made exclusively by trained social workers. The Trustees, however, interpreted their task differently. They were very aware that, first and foremost, it was important to relieve quickly the stress on families by providing practical help. The task of Family Fund was then done, unless a second application should be helpful in the future. If the family required continuing support, this was to be the responsibility of the statutory agencies and not of Family Fund itself. It was important that assessors should have experience of visiting families, but this service could be provided by a range of professions – social workers, health visitors or other experienced people – able to make quick decisions about the kind of help needed. What was important was the professional competence of the assessor from whatever background they came.

They were predominantly part-time and local and the knowledge they had of other resources which might be available in an area was to prove crucial, as we shall see when we examine signposting. Family Fund slowly built up a formidable body of assessors, dubbed by one civil servant 'The Laura Ashley Brigade' who, through practical support, were often able to 'shine a bit of light onto a dire situation', as one assessor put it. It was, as Ann Bond, an experienced assessor said, a 'humbling job' meeting families who had sometimes not spoken to anyone else about these issues, where the assessor often absorbed the challenges they faced. But it also had its amusing moments and Ann described visiting one family where the mother was bathing her small autistic son. Half way through the conversation she suddenly remembered she had her other children to collect from school and left Ann with both the baby and the bathwater!

Ann's point about being able to listen to families is a vital one. As she recounts

> *"We absorbed the aggro and grief by listening. We let people pour their hearts out."*

Families who have children with high levels of need don't always have the energy to fight despite, Ann argued, how brilliantly they cope. Ann describes how, when first appointed and with improvements in medicine, she would visit hospitals to meet premature babies and their parents. In one instance the parents were teenagers and faced a lot of opposition from staff who were disapproving and sceptical about their ability to cope. But Ann could see just how much they adored their baby, and with Ann's support and belief in them they thrived as a family. Ann's view as an assessor, in which she noted the change in referrals over the years – from requests for fridges and washing machines to IT and recreational activities – was that not only did Family Fund provide an 'economically sound model' but, through the local knowledge of assessors, a way of referring on for further help.

Inevitably, the assessors were visiting homes all over the UK and without Satnav, locations could sometimes be difficult to find. Writing in the Family Fund Trust Network News of May 1996, Dot Curtin, a Fund Regional Coordinator, described visiting a large council estate in the North of England:

'...somewhere I had been many times before and had never felt threatened or uncomfortable. Unfortunately, Family Fund had given me the wrong address. I duly wrote to the family saying I would be visiting, giving a time and date.

As arranged I knocked at the door at the appointed time, and was invited into the house by a man I presumed to be dad. At the door I explained who I was. He shut the front door behind me and directed me into the lounge and asked me to sit down while he shut the lounge door. It then became obvious he was alone and there wasn't a child living at his house. He then proceeded to tell me I was in the wrong house and he had asked me in, knowing I was not at the correct house. His manner was somewhat strange and female intuition told me to get out fast.

Somewhat shaken, I arrived at the right house – I did manage to get this information from him, only to find they kept a six foot python as a pet. I then wondered – was I more frightened of the python or the man!!!"

Sometimes, the role of the assessors has been expanded and, armed with the experience they had gained, they took on bigger roles within Family Fund. One example is Salena Begley who is now Family Fund's Partnership Manager in Scotland and is working to ensure that Family Fund is embedded within the fabric of voluntary and statutory organisations supporting households in Scotland. As Salena said, "I'm really proud to work for Family Fund".

In terms of Northern Ireland and a country still dealing with the legacy of the Troubles, Trustee Kate Fleck asserts that Family Fund is held in high esteem. It has been able to work across communities, the six trusts and five commissioning groups and is not just seen as an English organisation. Forming partnerships with policy groups, joining with others to campaign and being part of the advocacy for better services and being, as Kate states, 'there for the immediate'. The point that Family Fund is able to respond rapidly to a particular need is one that has been recognised elsewhere.

The establishment of the research element of Family Fund's work has supported the deepening of relations with Governments in all four nations. The role played by Family Fund in informing Government, supporting development of policy and communicating the challenges and issues that families make the Charity aware of, is essential in framing the attitudes to disability and support. Local partnerships with statutory and non-statutory bodies allow Family Fund to be seen as an organisation with 'on the ground' experience, not a remote, English-based charity but a human and local presence supporting families across all parts of the UK.

The independent review conducted in 2012 stressed the importance of home visits and stated that families noted that the empathy displayed by the Family Fund advisors set them apart from other organisations (The Moorhouse Review, 2012).

What has assisted the reviews and helped to set high standards throughout the organisation has been the systems of quality assurance that Family Fund established. Through telephone surveys, management visits and customer satisfaction questionnaires Family Fund has always been keen to evaluate how help is perceived. Families have not been slow to comment on the help they have received.

Behind the assessors was an increasingly sophisticated and organised support team, adapting to technology and changing patterns of delivery. The relentless movement from ledgers to card indexes, typewriters, word processors and eventually computers put the organisation through the same challenges that others had experienced. To those who feared that the first word processor would lead to redundancies can be added the words of Barbara Bradley, who came as a secretary to Family Fund in 1973 and recorded in 1999:

> *"Such were our fears of technology in those days. If only we had been given a glimpse into 1999".*

Two more characteristics of Fund staff has been their longevity and preparedness to think laterally. Elaine Pilmoor, who completes 32 years' service in 2023, only came for three weeks and records that one of the responsibilities she determined for herself was watering the flowers – which turned out to be artificial! The work experience offered by Family Fund to women from Askham Grange prison led to some being able to secure subsequent jobs. Alongside the introduction of computer technology, Family Fund has recruited an increasingly wide range of staff. The establishment of a First Contact team became particularly important during the Covid pandemic, with these colleagues answering 128,990 telephone calls in the period 2019–20.

Ben Calverley, who became the Director of Grant Services in 2013, has an interesting statistic which bridges the issue of assessment and signposting (to follow). In 2009, when Ben first joined Family Fund there were two staff answering the phones to potential grant recipients. During their lunch breaks and holidays, this function was taken on by other staff who were available. By the 2020s there were 27 specialist staff – because of the increased way that Family Fund understands why people contact it. They handle queries via the website, the telephone and email and in 2022 signposted to other services over 8,000 times.

Signposting – 'truly more than just a grant'

From the early days of assessor visits it quickly became evident that, for many families, this was the first real opportunity they had to talk about the challenges and rewards of caring for a child with disabilities, the lack of support from other agencies and the loneliness they sometimes faced. Parents and carers were often unaware of what help was available and to which organisations they could possibly turn. Alison Cowen's book *Taking Care*, first published by the Joseph Rowntree Trust in 1994, interviewed 20 families known to Family Fund on issues such as money matters, learning to cope with a child with disabilities, health and also housing. Despite the duty that social service departments have to publicise services, lack of information was high on the list of parents' complaints.

In a pattern that has characterised Family Fund during its 50 years' history, it was quick to look at how it could help families to access additional services and support. Soon Family Fund was helping to signpost to other services and, because assessors were usually local, they would know of help and support available. As one mother said...

> "The good thing about the Family Fund Trust is that you don't have to ask for information – it's just given to you."

For those who were making their applications via the telephone, the same helpful response was praised:

> *"The lovely person that rung me was very helpful and gave me lots of web pages and phone numbers for help and advice."*

This awareness that families are not always well informed has led Family Fund to develop an armoury of ways to keep carers up to date about national and sometimes local services. For several years Family Fund published a newsletter, called Network News, which was a combination of updates on relevant legislation, statutory and voluntary organisations and sources of additional help. This was followed by a steady stream of similar communications. Eleanor Barnes's *'The Family Fund and How it Helps'*, first published in 1980, was careful to include additional information about national organisations and, in 2004, Family Fund joined with the Norah Fry Research Centre, to produce *'All Together Better: A guide for families of a disabled child with complex health care needs'*.

A slight variation on this theme was a publication first produced in 1984 called *'After Age 16 – What Next?'* which eventually went through ten editions. Also published by the Joseph Rowntree Foundation and written by the Social Policy Research Unit at York University, it served two purposes:

- Firstly, it again signposted to help with services for young people with disabilities no longer able to access Family Fund grants

- Secondly, it was part of a growing movement within Family Fund to push for eligibility to be extended beyond the age of 16. By pointing to gaps in what was available, it helped enforce the point that Family Fund could help if the criteria were changed.

Financial realities for families

Families supported by Family Fund are, by definition, on low incomes in order to qualify for grants. In one study almost 2,000 families took part and the key findings were that such families are four times more likely to owe in excess of £10,000 in comparison with families who do not care for a disabled child. Their repayments on loans, credit cards and hire purchase agreements were 20 times the national average; and they spent, on average, £6,710 more than they earned. Recent research from Family Fund's Family Poll, considered later, confirms these findings remain relevant today.

Another factor which has made signposting more vital is the increasing complexity in the tax and benefits system itself. In 1984 there was a review of social security, announced as the most substantial changes since Beveridge, 40 years before. Launched by the-then minister, Norman Fowler, it was to investigate the whole of the supplementary benefits system, the allocation of benefits for children and young people and the system of benefits for people with disadvantages. It was followed by the introduction of the Social Fund schemes, implemented in 1987 and 1988 and replacing the former system of single payments of supplementary benefit.

In what is here only an illustrative account of changes to welfare benefits, reference should also be made to the Welfare Reform Act of 2012. This made alternatives to housing benefit, introduced Universal Credit, made changes to the Social Fund and phased out the Disability Living Allowance for Personal Independence Payments. These and other changes affected signposting in two ways: firstly, we see increasing references in the annual reports to benefits advice given by assessors during visits and on the phone; secondly, the increasing complexity of the welfare benefits system led to new strategic partnerships for Family Fund.

The 2011–12 Annual Report records that 8,785 families were visited at home by assessors. Nearly 10% increased their weekly income as a direct result of the visits. 46% of families had received advice from Family Fund about benefits, including the Disability Living Allowance. Similarly, the 2017–18 Annual Report refers to the First Contact team providing tax credit advice to 796 beneficiaries, resulting in significant financial benefits to families who had otherwise been likely to miss out on their entitlements. Families were able to claim up to £60 extra per week in tax credits, alongside sometimes thousands of pounds in unpaid back payments which were the result of changes in government policy.

The second development in this growing complexity in the tax and benefit system was a range of new partnerships with other and sometimes more specialised organisations. A pilot service with Contact a Family provided 1,493 families with additional support on issues such as access to benefits and, when ended in June 2017, was followed by a new partnership with the Citizens Advice Bureau (CAB). CAB had developed an information resource designed for their own advisors and covering all welfare issues from employment to benefits, housing and debts. The CAB made it available – under licence – to external organisations who also provide advice services to the public and whose services are compatible with the CAB's public benefit ethos. As such, Family Fund was a natural fit.

Similarly, Family Fund linked up with Turn 2 Us, a national charity that helps people living in poverty and provides information and support about welfare benefits and other financial support. In these and similar schemes – like those described earlier that brought together IT with financial training – Family Fund has created comprehensive databases of information in order to help families navigate the complex world of financial support.

It would be difficult to calculate the additional financial support over the years that Family Fund has made possible for families, through signposting. It is equally unlikely to have been part of the original intentions when Family Fund was established but it is another demonstration of the way Family Fund has evolved, through listening and responding to what families need.

Interview with Kizzy – second generation of Fund support

I already knew about Family Fund. My mum, Anne, has a serious sight impairment and, as children, we had some support, since my three siblings also have a visual impairment. We were very poor and couldn't afford very much. As a result of grants from Family Fund we went away on holidays to deepest, darkest Scotland and to other places. We would never have been able to afford this otherwise.

John, my son, has autism and some developmental delays. He needed specialist toys and Family Fund were fantastic. Through the toys I was able to bond, non-verbally, with John. I began to understand him much better. I began to see small bits of him developing. He was fascinated by one of those rain tubes which the grant allowed us to buy and I remember he had a wooden version of Whack-a-Mole which he loved. And if ever there was a problem with the toys we could always get them changed.

The second grant was a subscription to a leisure centre. John has a huge fear of water. He hates it and I wanted to help him. So, twice a week we'd go and I'd just sit with him near the edge of the pool. The year's entry pass also meant that his two siblings, aged 11 and 13 could come as well. As John and I would sit on the edge of the pool they would swim over and bring him things to throw in. Now he is able to go in up to his waist and it is getting better. The year's free entry was fantastic.

John has an individual education plan and goes to a special school on a bus. He is in a small class and he is thriving. Both of my parents are now rehabilitation officers, so I was aware of the sorts of support that would be available.

I think Family Fund is a fantastic cause. I wish they would do more fundraising so that they could help even more families. Now the children are growing I have begun training to be a nurse. I'm doing some courses before going to university. I expect I shall end up in children's nursing.

Chapter 6

Fifty Years Of Keeping Pace With Health, Education and Family Profiles

Health and education services have been transformed in the last 50 years. New medication, treatments, and debates about segregated versus integrated education have led to a sea change in the way children with additional needs are treated. For Family Fund this has involved paying close attention to government policies across the four UK nations, detailed listening to the experiences of carers and a nimbleness and willingness to adapt and change services.

The health of children

If we take health, the introduction of vaccination programmes, the establishment of neonatal intensive care units, improved responses to premature babies and a tsunami of new pharmacological drugs have transformed health care for children. It is scarcely possible to over emphasise the changes to children's health that have taken place since Family Fund was established. The ability of Family Fund to keep pace with developments in paediatric care is one of the many reasons for its success.

As discussed in Chapter 2 ,and if we return to the Department of Health and Social Security's definition in 1973 of eligibility for Family Fund, it was for families:

> *'who have children under 16 who in the opinion of the Trust are very severely congenitally handicapped, whether physically (including the totally blind or deaf) or mentally'.*

As we saw earlier, this definition was deliberately framed so that it went wider but also included children affected by thalidomide. But this was a potential problem for the Joseph Rowntree Foundation, with the Trustees realising that in attempting to define both 'severely' and 'congenitally handicapped' they would easily be courting controversy. As far as the government was concerned, they were keen that it should benefit a limited number of children. As we saw, in the next two to three years there were several new definitions which fine-tuned the criteria. So, in December 1974, the requirement to restrict assistance to congenital conditions was dropped, so that medical eligibility became dependent upon the *severity* rather than the *cause* of the disability. No apology is made for repeating this part of Family Fund's history because the battles won in the early stages were to have profound significance. This is particularly the case given the increasing complexity in the types of both physical and mental disability facing children.

By 1976 the criteria accepted by Family Fund included the loss of two or more limbs, asthma, cerebral palsy, cystic fibrosis, epilepsy, severe hearing and sight loss, muscular dystrophy, spina bifida, Down's syndrome and what was then defined as 'mental sub normality'.

We learn that between the establishment of Family Fund in March 1973 and April 1976, when Jonathan Bradshaw's survey of the first three years ended (Bradshaw,1980), 'mental sub normality' represented the biggest category of applicants (32.3%) followed by spina bifida and hydrocephalus (18.1%), cerebral palsy (16.9%) and deafness (4.7%). These categories may already seem surprising, given the original definition of Family Fund's purpose and help to demonstrate that, from its origins, Family Fund was able to respond to parents' needs, rather than be bound by a rigid definition which excluded those most in need of support.

So how has the pattern of application changed between 1976 and 2023? To understand this, it is necessary to touch on changes to paediatrics and also the nature of childhood disability. Some conditions reveal themselves from birth, while others only begin to be disabling later in childhood. Other disabilities, such as those resulting from accidents, can occur at any time – hence, the initial importance of widening the criteria beyond congenital conditions. During this period medical technology has had a major impact on the survival rates of children born with a disabling condition or on those born very prematurely. At the same time, the last 50 years has seen a gradual movement away from long-term residential care to a policy of keeping children in the community and preferably with their families.

What emerges very strongly since the late 1960s and up to the present day has been the ways in which a raft of vaccination programmes has transformed children's health care. Measles, a significant cause of disability and hearing loss was first tackled with a vaccine introduced into the UK in 1968. A Rubella vaccine was licensed a year later and one for mumps in 1988. Mumps had been a significant cause of deafness in children and also could lead to meningitis and encephalitis. On the heels of these were haemophilus influenza type B (HIB) in 1992, meningococcus C vaccine in 1999, the B vaccine in 2015 and the pneumococcal vaccine in 2001. All of these played a part in reducing risks of meningitis, cerebral palsy, learning disabilities and deafness.

Alongside these pharmacological innovations was the development of neonatal intensive care. This encouraged a wealth of diagnostic techniques in the 1970s and 1980s, such as ultrasound imaging, magnetic resonance spectroscopy and the setting up of special care baby units in major maternity hospitals.

This combination of vaccine programmes and improvements to neonatal care have jointly had huge effects on the decline in neonatal mortality rates. By the 1980s, 80% of babies with less than 33 weeks gestation were doing well and, particularly over the last 25 years, the prospects of babies who are born prematurely, have congestant anomalies requiring surgery, or who develop illnesses after birth have improved greatly. All of these developments were, of course, accompanied by better infection prevention and improvements in pharmacological drugs. The other side of this – directly relevant to Family Fund – is that increased technology, keeping younger and younger babies alive, often means that parents and carers have to cope with more complicated medical needs.

Moving forward from the Bradshaw survey, the Joseph Rowntree Foundation's annual reports on Family Fund continued to look at trends in applications across the UK. It found an increase in specific diagnoses, chiefly in relation to genetic disorders and, unsurprisingly given what we have seen above about new vaccination programmes, a decline in applications relating to spina bifida and congenital rubella. There had been a five-fold increase in applications relating to asthma and skin disorders while requests linked to leukaemia and cancer had doubled. By 1992 the highest category was non-specific learning disability/developmental delay (16.1%) followed by cerebral palsy (10.7%) and asthma (7.4%).

But these figures also revealed some variations between the four UK countries.

- In Northern Ireland, spina bifida, Down's syndrome and asthma figured significantly with also a high incidence of disability due to burns.

- Both Scotland and Wales recorded cases of Perthes' disease of the hip, affecting the mobility of children and, in Wales, this was accompanied by cancer, leukaemia, heart conditions and scoliosis.

- In parts of England there were higher incidences of illness affecting the circulatory system, autism and deafness.

Across the UK congenital rubella had declined, because of the immunisation programme among teenage girls and both spina bifida and Down's syndrome applications were down; the latter due to pre-natal screening programmes. Lastly, Family Fund was seeing more incidence of cancer, leukaemia and autism and referrals for diabetes had also increased. Aggregating all four UK countries, the top three prevalent conditions between 1998 and 2003 were learning difficulties, cerebral palsy and autism.

Changes to the prevalence of certain conditions has inevitably affected the types of grants made by Family Fund; numbers of children with disabilities have also fluctuated. In the last decade the proportion of disabled children has increased from 6% (2010–11) of the childhood population to 9% (2020–21). Between 2015 and 2021 the number of children with an Education Health and Care Plan (EHCP) or Special Educational Needs (SEN) has increased from 14.4% to 15.8% of the childhood population, which equated to an additional 180,000 children. Improvements in neo-natal care, outlined above, have resulted in more pre-term survivors (between 22 and 26 weeks) where, in some cases, there are risks of later health problems. In certain areas – including Attention Deficit Hyperactivity Disorder (ADHD), autism, complex needs, learning disability, and visual impairment – there has been a rise in the number of children diagnosed. As well as improved care in the early weeks of life, some of the increases might also be down to changes in diagnostic criteria. So ADHD increased by 167% between 1998 and 2010 and diagnoses of autism by 62% between 2015 and 2021. A review of primary care records (between 1998 and 2018) for people with a diagnosis of autism recorded a 787% increase with more boys than girls likely to be diagnosed and the average age of diagnosis increasing from 9.6 years in 1998 to 14.5 years in 2018 (cf Disabled Children's Partnership 2022).

In a category on complex need and life limiting/threatening conditions, the Disabled Children's Partnership analysis reports a 50% increase within the last decade. In the same decade, the proportion of those discharged with supplementary oxygen has increased by 7%. Both hearing and visual impairment have also increased, with a 33% increase in hearing impaired children between 2011 and 2019 and Blind UK reporting a 9% increase in children with visual impairment in England and Wales between 2006 and 2014. Similarly, pupils with a primary diagnosis of multi-sensory impairment increased by 65% between 2015 and 2021 and those children with a primary diagnosis of physical disability increased by 183% again between 2015 and 2021.

A number of factors have affected these growing statistics. Not only has the number of children surviving previously life-threatening conditions increased, but the length of time they are subsequently living has lengthened. Furthermore, there is a larger proportion of children with more than one disability, such as ADHD and autistic spectrum conditions. Perhaps not surprisingly, as evidenced by the cross referencing of Family Fund data with the WIMD referred to earlier, the prevalence of life-limiting conditions is highest among children living in the most deprived areas.

The Disabled Children's Partnership research predicts that the number of children with complex and life limiting needs will rise by 2030 to 67–84 children per 10,000 (more than three times the rate in 2001).

To bring this account of health changes up to date, we need to factor in the effects of the Covid pandemic. It is still too early to provide a definitive analysis of the impacts of the pandemic, but evidence is indicating that the mental health of children has been, in some cases, severely affected. Deprived of school and the company of friends and, in the case of children with disabilities, no longer able to obtain additional support, access to some medical facilities or therapy, it is easy to speculate that this is likely to find its way through to additional referrals to Family Fund. Indeed, the evidence is building up to show that this has already happened. Add to this the huge increase in conditions such as autism and ADHD and Family Fund's grant programme is likely to be stretched further.

We are a long way from the early JRF analysis which calculated a maximum of about 100,000 children who might require support from Family Fund. If nothing else, the above analysis reveals that, in terms of medical needs alone, Family Fund is required even more than ever. There has not only been a necessity to ensure that the core grant from the four UK governments stretched further and further but that changes in patterns of disability were reflected in the kind of grants made. Perhaps the biggest example of this, which we have explored elsewhere, is the way in which computer technology has transformed the assistance available to a wide range of children with physical and mental disabilities.

Changes in education

As we have seen, Family Fund needed to be nimble, in order to keep pace with developments in health care. The same is equally true of educational change and reform in the last 50 years. For Family Fund it has meant actively keeping the concerns of children and young people with special educational needs and disability (SEND) central to governments' educational policies and lobbying either alone or with other organisations to improve opportunities and outcomes for children. For just as families with SEND children experience additional expenditure on basics like heating, housing and clothing, so they also undergo increased levels of social and education exclusion. This has been made more acute by the national shortage of special educational provision.

If we were to admit a fairly large simplification and summary of educational policy in the last fifty years, it would be characterised in all four UK countries by a debate about the greater inclusion of children with SEND into mainstream education on the one hand and, on the other, a movement for more specialist educational provision. For the purposes of the last fifty years in which Family Fund has operated, the debate was opened by the Warnock report, five years after the Trust was established. It was 'an enquiry into the education of handicapped children and young people'. Warnock provided the first comprehensive review of special educational needs and became a landmark event for parents and children. It covered educational provision in England, Scotland and Wales, reviewing educational provision up to the entry into employment. Warnock recognised that there were children who were included into mainstream schools – what she described as 'special educational provision in ordinary schools' and this, to some extent influenced her thinking.

Interestingly, forty years later, when Mary Warnock gave evidence to the Education Committee's consideration of 'special educational needs and disabilities' (2018) she expressed grave doubts about inclusivity. She took the view that for some children mainstream education was not appropriate and particularly singled out children with autism. She argued that there were a considerable number of children who would never be integrated into larger schools. Problems, she argued, increased with the size of the school and while primary education could accommodate SEND children, secondary schools often struggled.

Asked further to reflect on the success of the earlier report, Warnock said that in 1981, when the *Education Act*'s stated government's intention 'to make provision with respect to children with special educational needs' was enacted, it also corresponded with major cuts to public services. The result was a major blow to the implementation of Warnock's recommendations. But it did give parents new rights in relation to special needs, urged the inclusion of SEND children into mainstream schools, and introduced a system of 'statementing' children to give them entitlement to special educational support.

One of the major significances of Warnock for Family Fund, amidst the ebb and flow of inclusion versus specialist provision, was that at least the needs of SEND children were beginning to be talked about. This allowed Family Fund to join other organisations in amplifying the call for better provision and increased resources. Increasingly too, as we have discussed in Chapter 5, Family Fund's staff found themselves signposting carers to other sources of help, offering advice both about getting a diagnosis for the children and how to go to tribunals to overturn decisions. The other development, which fitted in perfectly with the basic ethos of Family Fund, was an increasing willingness to listen to the voice of carers. This was assisted by the Lamb Inquiry in 2009, which aimed at improving communication and engagement with parents and strongly made the point that parents' voices should be listened to. For Family Fund this has always been a guiding principle. In 1994, 15 years before the Lamb Inquiry, Family Fund had published 'Taking Care', exclusively raising issues of concern from carers themselves.

To complete this roll call of legislation, the Government introduced the *Children and Families Act* in 2014 and the SEND review in 2022. The 2014 legislation introduced personal budgets, both to give families with an education, health and care plan more control and also requiring education, health and social care to work together more closely. However, as Warnock had said of the *1981 Education Act*, it still remained to be properly financed and implemented.

Lastly, the 2022 SEND review started from three critical premises. It was in response to the widespread belief that the system for SEND children was failing to deliver.

- Firstly, navigating the SEND system was not a positive experience.

- Secondly, outcomes for children and young people with SEND were seen to be worse than for peers across every measure.

- Thirdly, the system was not seen as financially sustainable.

All of which point to the distance still to be travelled if we are to provide a service for carers and SEND children commensurate with that available to other children.

This brief summary provides an educational backcloth against which Family Fund has operated. The response of Family Fund has been characteristically positive: a combination of signposting carers to help, lobbying – either separately or with other organisations – to improve services and, through grants, providing practical educational support.

Perhaps the greatest demonstration of this practical support has come through IT. As we saw in Chapter 3, Family Fund became involved in the Golden Freeway project, offering an electronic support network for boys with Duchenne muscular dystrophy. The scheme was so successful as an educational tool that Family Fund decided to widen the criteria for assistance and from February 2003 requests from families for computer equipment were met by Family Fund. Such grants sometimes helped with communication, allowed children to play, and in the context of education, helped with the integration of children by accessing the same technology experienced by other children. That the spirit of the age, in theory at least, was for greater inclusion within education offered some support to the whole encompassing ethos of Family Fund itself.

What could not be predicted was the onset of Covid and the huge implications this would especially have for the families of SEND children. Not only did it mean that 'normal' education ceased but families were denied the essential break they often needed while looking after their children. Although Family Fund developed initiatives during lockdown, like the 'Break At Home' scheme, to replace cancelled holidays that families had often been desperate to take, and continued to provide IT equipment to assist with learning, the pressure on children with disabilities has probably been incalculable. As we shall see elsewhere, Covid also led to another major change in the way Family Fund operated.

Family profiles

Against the backdrop of considerable change – both to children's health and education – during the course of Family Fund's 50 year history, what do we know about the supported families themselves? As we have seen, when Family Fund was first set up in 1973, it was calculated that it would support about 100,000 families. It was in the light of this information that a Note of Guidance was issued in April 1973, making it clear that there would not be an assessment based on income:

> *'With regard to the economic circumstances of a family it is not intended to introduce a form of means test. The panel will however have to be satisfied from the social reports provided that the financial circumstances of a family, in relation to their commitments are such that recourse to Family Fund is justified.'*

This was further clarified in May the same year, when it was repeated that no form of means testing should be employed but that when considering the family's level of income, it was necessary to take into account the impact of the child's disability on the way of life of the family in comparison with their peers. In the early days of Family Fund, when administration was minimal, not only would a means test have added enormously to the complexity of the process, but it was also recognised that even relatively well-off families might experience difficulty in finding the money for some of the more expensive items provided by Family Fund.

However, initial estimates of a finite number of applicants to Family Fund proved far from the mark and by the mid-1980s a level of family income for grant applications had been introduced. Since then, the cut-off point has been periodically reassessed.

In his survey of the first three years of Family Fund, Jonathan Bradshaw (1980) looked at the age, class, employment of wives and husbands and wider composition of grant applicants. Beginning with age, Bradshaw found that between 1973 and 1976 the age distribution of children was fairly even between 1 and 15, although families with very small children tended to be underrepresented. In terms of social class distribution, the majority were manual workers, with few of the wives of applicants to Family Fund able to go out to work to supplement family income. As we might expect, those able to go into full time work were lower in numbers than the already limited group able to obtain part-time employment. When looking at family composition, Bradshaw concluded that single-parent families and large families with disabled children were more represented than smaller families; this was also confirmed in the 1973 *General Household Survey*. Bradshaw found that the economic circumstances of families applying to Family Fund were lower than for the population as a whole 'and probably lower than the population of all families with disabled children'. (This latter group would, of course, include many families where the degree of disability made them ineligible to apply.)

Moving on, a significant staging point was the 30th anniversary of Family Fund, in 2003, when Family Fund was again keen to see how the profile of applicants had changed. The majority (60.8%) of applicants were in two-parent families with at least one parent employed (56.9%). It was largely mothers who were not in paid employment. One in ten did not have English as their first language and Family Fund was providing telephone translation to support applications. Also, advisors in Wales conducted interviews with Welsh speaking families in their native language. The largest group of applicants were white, at 84%, with Pakistani applicants making up 5% of the total and smaller percentages of Black African, Caribbean, Indian and Chinese applicants.

The 2005–6 Annual Report revealed that 90% of families supported by Family Fund had an income from employment below the UK average and nearly a third lived in poverty. We may speculate that the challenge of caring for a child with a disability both limited the hours they could work and the kinds of jobs available. The 2013 *Moorhouse Review* quoted independent research that families with no disabled children had an average total weekly income of £543, those with a disabled child £475 and for a lone parent with a disabled child, the income was even lower, at £300.

Family Fund has been consistently concerned to ensure that it both represented the changing ethnicity of the wider UK population and reached out to communities less familiar with what it had to offer. In 2011–12 the Annual Report records that of those completing the ethnicity identification form, 83% identified as white, with the remaining 17% of families recording themselves as Asian/Asian British (8%), Black/Black British (6%), mixed race (2%) and Chinese (1%). The *Moorhouse Review*, referenced above, conducted a survey, in 2013, of 2,848 families and revealed that the proportion of respondents who came from a black or minority ethnic community, accessing Family Fund, was higher than the national average (14% of survey respondents, compared with 9% of the national population). For Scotland, Wales and Northern Ireland the proportions were the same as the national average. The review concluded that Family Fund was reaching an 'adequate' proportion of BME families in each of the countries. We shall return to this when we look later at current data.

The Fund also produced a series of Activity reports in 2002–3 on Northern Ireland, Scotland and Wales, and continue to do so. In Wales 40% of grant recipients were in local authority rented accommodation and 36% in owner occupied properties. 87% of mothers were not in paid employment and 95% were on income support. In Northern Ireland the per centage of mothers not in paid employment was one per centage point higher at 88% and the majority of grants were made in the Eastern Region of the country. In Scotland, the highest proportion of families helped lived in Glasgow, 57% were in two parent families and 42% with a single parent. Here, 86% of mothers were not in paid employment, 59% were in rented and local authority accommodation and 97% of families were on income support.

What the above demonstrates is an organisation which, from its outset, has been keen to ensure that it was reaching out to those in greatest need. We have seen elsewhere how this information has been put to best use to, for example, offer support in budgeting and ensure that literature about the Fund is available in a range of languages. As we now see, Family Fund has taken even bigger strides in the last three years to produce sophisticated data which, in turn, has helped to inform effective grant making.

The Database and Family Polls

The reader who has got this far may recall that one of the foresighted ideas developed by Family Fund from its earliest days was the gathering of data. The task was given to the University of York, and Family Fund now has an unparalleled source of anonymous information on the health, economic background and social circumstances of the families they have supported. From that very first grant to the family in Wales requiring transport for their daughter's operation, where names, income, family composition and reason for the request were recorded has grown a rich source of material, used for epidemiological purposes, by a range of organisations. Now, as well as composition of the family household, the database anonymously records ethnic origin, country or region, the current housing situation, information about the disabled child and associated costs, levels of debt, household income, savings and debt, the family's use of new technology, external and financial support, and comparisons with the previous year. All of this has been made possible by a strengthening of the research staff within Family Fund and, as we shall see, an ability to interrogate the data not only to extract quantitative but also invaluable qualitative material.

So what do we now know about the families who are currently receiving grants? Well, based on 2020–21 data, the majority of families have one child with a disability, although, for a quarter this stretched to two; 43% are in single households; 57% are across multi-adult households (often with another generation) and, in 44% of households, the family also contained an adult with a disability. The biggest percentage of disabled children are between the ages of 5 and 10 (39% are female and 61% male). With this, as with other statistics, it is a UK-wide averaged figure so, for example, in Wales only 25% are female and 75% male. When asked how the disability or illness affected the child, 78% said socially or behaviourally, 76% through learning, understanding or concentration and 61% through challenges over communication.

When we turn to ethnic origin, across the UK 80% identify as white British, although when broken down across the four UK nations this varied from 89% in Scotland and 91% in Wales to 63% in Northern Ireland. In terms of other ethnic groups, 4% defined themselves as Black or Black African, 2% from Pakistan and 1% Asian or Asian British-Bangladeshi.

The largest per centage live in rented accommodation (52% across the whole of the UK but up to 60% in Scotland), with only 20% buying their own homes with a mortgage. 58% were not in paid employment, and the largest per centage was on an income of less than £10,000 a year. Having a child with a disability left a large per centage unable to work, because of the extra demands on their time required to deliver care. 91% were in receipt of disability benefits across the UK. A consistent theme is the way in which a range of regular household costs are increased because of extra expenditure needed for a child with a disability. This ranges from items such as beds and bedding, cleaning products and clothing, to emergency costs, food and groceries, hospital visits, tablets, computers and toiletries. Additionally, there is little or no statutory support to purchase the often expensive specialist equipment including specific toys, play equipment and additional educational material needed to allow these children the same chances as their peers. It is not surprising that, for many families, the only way to survive is by incurring debt, whether this is through credit cards, loans, or rent and energy bill arrears. The average level of debt is £5,592 per family with half of the sample declaring that the amount of debt is £500 higher than it was twelve months ago. Worryingly, about a third also believed that it was likely they would have more borrowings and debts in the next twelve months.

The period covered in this analysis is what Family Fund's 2020–21 Annual Report refers to as 'a year like no other'. Families coped with Covid, school lockdowns, reduced employment and, as a result for many, lower income. As we turn to the Family Poll, we shall see that all of this led to a pessimism not only about the levels of disposable income which would be available in the future but, as a result, the quality of life for the families.

From this database, captured through the grants application process, researchers have progressed to look in greater detail at a smaller sample, a representative group which is typical of families on low incomes raising disabled children across the UK. From a sample of 1,066 families it is possible to gain an unparalleled glimpse into the lives of the families – their fears, expectations and the sacrifices that they often make on a daily basis. So, for example, on average, they spend 62 hours a week caring for their disabled child, receiving little more than one hour a week extra care, outside of the child's educational setting. 68% of the sample calculated that they are worse off than before the pandemic and that their bills had increased by more than £100 a month. As a result, 90% were struggling or falling behind with household bills, whether this was council tax, energy, IT, rent, mortgage or water bills. 71% had no savings and no longer felt able to commit to regular savings for extra things like specialist toys, equipment or even therapies for their child.

With debts increasing, families responded that they were being forced to cut back on adult clothes, energy and transport costs and, in some cases, food for the adults. There was an increasing use of food banks; furniture needing replacing was left in situ and carers had little left to spend on themselves. In a continuation of this qualitative data, a third admitted to experiencing loneliness 'often or always' and felt that the most practical kinds of support would be day trips out, to get away, energy vouchers, cash and food grants. And yet, families still strived to make sure that their disabled child had a tablet or computer, that special occasions and birthdays were properly celebrated and that the children were adequately provided with fruit and vegetables every day.

Reinforcing Family Fund's focus on signposting, families said they needed information on other grants they might obtain or advice about mental health and wellbeing and ways of reducing everyday costs. For a group of carers for whom life is routinely challenging, the pandemic has had profound effects on their and their children's lives. As we turn to Family Fund and the next 50 years we might sadly conclude that families with disabled children need support more than ever and the need for Family Fund is as great, if not greater, than it was in 1973.

Jo Spear and son Archie, 2010s

I discovered Family Fund when our washing machine and oven broke in quick succession. I had started looking at a payment plan to replace them when our SEND coordinator suggested Family Fund. I phoned the helpline and they were immediately welcoming. They certainly helped and also listened to my mini rant about the washing machine!

They explained that someone might come out to see me but the next thing was a letter saying we could have the money for a replacement. And the good news was that Family Fund have also negotiated a five-year warranty, so you have some peace of mind.

Since then, I have always had a wish to pay back Family Fund for the help they gave us. During lockdown we needed an iPad for Archie, to assist him with some school work and, again, they helped. So I wanted to talk about my positive experiences. With everyone I speak to at Family Fund it's as if I have known them for twenty years. Every person has been fabulous. It's not just a charity that gives you things. They support the whole family. What other charity does that? They just help. And they involve you in other ways. For example, in a focus group on the SEND review, so you can contribute your views and have your say. They have certainly helped us out at critical times and they have always listened. They love their jobs and it feels like a family. They help with respite – whether this is days out or holidays – and then there is the community element as well.

There is never what I call a 'Monday blues' situation. Everyone appears happy to be doing their job and as a result they have had a huge impact on my family and on other families. And it is incredible how many people they reach. They also use good suppliers and there is always an integrity behind what they do. But they are constantly striving to do more.

Archie is now six. I have three children, another son with special needs and a daughter as well. And Family Fund don't just look at the one child but at the whole family. I'd say that 'family' is at the centre of what they do. And they know how much a child with disabilities impacts on the whole family. I also get the emails and newsletter so they help me to keep in touch, assist with signposting and often have links to other organisations. They make it easier to get other services. The website is always clear and there is lots of information.

It really is important to realise how they support the family. They are open and always honest. They start off by saying 'What do you need?', 'What is it you want?', and if they can't help with a particular thing then 'What else might help?' They just go out of their way for you.

Chapter 7

The Next Fifty Years

Family Fund began life as what might be described as an experiment in social policy. It was a test to see whether a voluntary body might have advantages in both caring and efficiency in the delivery of government funding. The next 50 years demonstrated what a wise, if at the time pragmatic, decision this was. Rightly, the governments have insisted on periodic and independent reviews of Family Fund, to measure its effectiveness. The first of these took place in 1985 and was then repeated, albeit in different formats, in 1993, 1999, 2012, 2019 and 2022. Just as the kind of support granted reflects changes in education and children's health care so, too, the reviews mirror the way in which grant distribution and accountability have developed over 50 years.

Independent reviews

The first review, independently conducted in 1985 by Korda and Company, was preoccupied with the Family Fund's move from paper filing and accounts to electric typewriters! Family Fund, at that time, had a limited number of what they described as 'memory typewriters' which meant that substantial numbers of standard letters were being typed from scratch. Korda recommended major investment in a central computer system – two 'minicomputers' back-to-back to protect Family Fund against the risk of system failure. The review went on to conclude that Family Fund was well run: there were 29 staff and the grant makers each dealt with the equivalent of four and a half payments per day. This amounted to 29,124 payments per year by 1984. Searching for a comparison, Korda looked at insurance companies dealing with claims and concluded that Family Fund was achieving a high level of productivity. They describe the ethos of the Family Fund as 'unusual if not unique'. The staff, they argued, combined a very practical appreciation of the stresses under which their 'clients' laboured, with a total commitment to provide the best possible service to them.

Another independent review was carried out in 1993, which reviewed Family Fund compared to other forms of government support, such as the Social Fund, the Disability Living Allowance, Motability, hospital visiting costs and, at a local authority level, the Chronically Sick and Disabled Person's Act. It concluded that the aim of Family Fund – to complement these statutory services – was well met, which is an argument we will return to when we look at criticism of Family Fund itself.

In 1999 the Department of Health decided to do a review of Family Fund, the first since it had become registered as a separate charity three years earlier. By then Family Fund was making 100,297 grants a year from 78,401 applications; a thirty three per cent increase in the number of applications over the previous five years. The Department speculated that this increase was attributable to constraints in government funding and a pattern we see repeated over fifty years, that Family Fund filled the gap where assistance from other statutory bodies and local authorities was lacking. The report was, like Korda before it, strong on the cost effectiveness of Family Fund itself. Family visits were seen as both highly valued and cost effective and the Department noted that 90 pence in every pound was allocated to direct grants. Furthermore, through the discounts on domestic appliance procurements, Family Fund had made savings of nearly £700,000 – the equivalent to purchasing an additional 3,100 washing machines at 1998/99 prices. Workloads had risen by one third since the mid 1990s, response times had come down considerably and, to mark progress since 1985, Family Fund was attributed with having 'a high quality IT system'. Gone were the electronic typewriters, paper systems and major duplication in the way in which grants were delivered. Lastly, the report flagged up the need for Family Fund to prepare for a much greater degree of devolution between the four nations. But an over-riding observation of the Trust's philosophy and purpose is one of being established ahead of its time.

The 2013 review, conducted by the Moorhouse Consortium, on behalf of the Department for Education, was the most detailed of the reviews in its consideration of those families and children Family Fund supported. A starting point was whether the Family Fund model was the right approach to supporting low income families of severely disabled children. It recorded that Family Fund was the largest grant giving organisation helping families with disabled children. With 187 'advisors', making the grants, it made 96,397 grants in 2011/12 to 59,166 families, with an average award of £564. They noted that Family Fund Trading had been set up in 2008 and described Family Fund variously as 'an investment model – to support disabled children and help reduce the number of families falling into costly crisis' and as being 'run as a business with a charity angle'. The review calculated that the cost of looking after a disabled child was three times higher than for other children, when factors like specialist toys, transport and extra support were taken into consideration. The review also commented favourably on the links that Family Fund had made with organisations like the Council for Disabled Children, Contact a Family and Grandparents Plus and provided a breakdown of the most prevalent disabilities. In 2011/12, when the survey was done, the most common disabilities were children on the autistic spectrum, those with learning disabilities and hearing or communication difficulties. Less than 5% of the children helped had cerebral palsy, heart disease, Down's syndrome or epilepsy. Overall the review concluded that Family Fund was well placed to carry out 'its unique role – representing the best package of low-risk, efficiency and greatest impact on outcomes'.

Family Fund as an 'ineffectual gesture'

It is remarkable how little criticism Family Fund has encountered in its 50 years. The JRF Trustees' initial concerns that Family Fund would become implicated in the thalidomide scandal proved groundless and very soon the range and flexibility of grant giving helped establish Family Fund's credibility. However, writing in *The Times* in 1973, Peter Townsend described the setting up of Family Fund as an 'ineffectual gesture'. It needed to be part of a comprehensive strategy with expenditure thirty times the figure of £3million, if families were to receive adequate financial support. Townsend renewed this criticism with a review of Jonathon Bradshaw's then newly published book on Family Fund in the journal *Tribune* (26th September 1980). He saw Family Fund as 'another vehicle of social control', not part of a comprehensive and coherent policy for children with disabilities; he repeated the claim that such a plan would have cost many millions of pounds if it were to respond fully to the needs of families.

To some extent Jonathan Bradshaw had anticipated these criticisms in his own book. Family Fund, he argued, which was flexible and to some extent discretionary, can only be justified as an adjunct to a system of clearly delineated rights, based on principles of equity. In other words, Family Fund had a valuable role to play, but only as an addition to what the state could provide through benefits and other kinds of support. Eloquently, the mother of a four-year-old boy with autism expressed the contribution Family Fund can make:

> "Your organisation changes lives, non-judgmentally, improving people's lives. Maybe that isn't world-changing but it improves individual families' worlds."

A very large gap has been filled by Family Fund as, amongst other things, a broker, a coordinator of other grant-making programmes and, increasingly, as a service provider.

It was never intended to be a substitute for the welfare state but, as we have seen, the various ways in which Family Fund has used the grant programme to achieve leverage in other areas have amplified the contribution it has made. This has not simply been in influencing for change, often in the area of welfare benefits for families, but developing new programmes, as a result of the additional income raised. Discounts and rebates from the bulk purchasing of some items – which in turn allowed Family Fund to award more grants, extra grants from other foundations and grant making trusts, and over the last decade the increasing income from FFBS and fundraising – have ensured that Family Fund's reach has extended beyond simply administering the funds made available by the four UK governments. All of this access to other funding would not have been possible if Family Fund had remained as part of a single government programme. Two of many examples illustrate this most vividly:

- *Tired All the Time* sprang from the direct experience of parents and carers talking about the relentless challenge and pressures of caring for children and young people whose sleep patterns were often badly disturbed. It led to a report which was launched in all four of the UK parliaments and the establishment of a Sleep Hub offering local and national support and help. In Scotland it was linked to the launch of a respite care programme, offering help for families who often badly needed a break.

- Similarly, while many charities would have been content to provide iPads to families in need, Family Fund saw this as a starting point for a range of initiatives. If you give out iPads you need to make sure that families and children are making the most of them and also having some training in how to use them. Hence the launch of the iPad summer schools. Since some families expressed difficulty in budgeting, why not link iPads to IT training in how to assist with budgeting? It is this combination of imagination and lateral thinking that has characterised Family Fund's work.

Alongside Family Fund's ability to think creatively has been the determination not to 'take the King's shilling', but to retain its independence. Reference has already been made to the offer in 1987 from the Department of Health and Social Security for Family Fund to accept £5 million a year, for three years, to administer a fund which would support several hundred severely disabled people, living in their own homes, who were denied financial support within the social security system. Here, Family Fund would have become a direct substitute for statutory support and – referring back to the earlier debate about the additional nature of Fund grants – it would have become part of the delivery of mainline, statutory help.

It was Harold MacMillan who said that what changed politics was 'events, dear boy, events'. Three major sets of events have also forced Family Fund to show all of the flexibility which fortunately has characterised its last 50 years: devolution, the coronavirus and the cost-of-living crisis. Like many organisations Family Fund was forced, by the spread of coronavirus to modify its working patterns overnight. But grants still needed to be made and the pressures on families were, if anything, greater, as they coped with schools closing, all leisure centres no longer open, restricted support from health and social care staff and added difficulties in accessing health provision.

Recently, as coronavirus restrictions have been eased, families on low incomes helped by Family Fund have been hit hardest by cost-of-living hikes. Not only have food and other essentials become more expensive, but so, specifically, has heating and electricity. This is particularly difficult for families who may need to maintain higher temperatures for sick children or for the extra costs of running specialist equipment which their children may require.

Lastly, in this list of 'events' has been the willingness of Family Fund to respond to devolution. Family Fund has always seen itself as a four nations' organisation. In 1998 the distribution of the grants was devolved to the four UK nations and Family Fund has been able to respond to the sometimes very different priorities for families that have developed across England, Scotland, Northern Ireland and Wales. With devolution has come the ability for Family Fund to take part in policy debates about future needs and to forge new relationships with other voluntary sector partners in every area of the UK.

In terms of awareness raising, a short film released in 2022 of TV personality and *Masterchef* judge Greg Wallace meeting the White family starkly illustrated the challenges of caring for a disabled child and facing the consequences of rising food and energy bills. Under the banner of Family Fund's partnership with McCain focused on supporting families to come together and enjoy mealtimes, this is a campaign which has the possibility of bringing the daily challenges of families with a disabled child to the awareness of a much wider audience. Family Fund has truly become a four-nation organisation with what marketing experts would refer to as much increased brand awareness.

With an increasingly sophisticated set of metrics for measuring those who receive grants, Family Fund is not standing still. A recent analysis of 2020/21 Family Resources Survey data has worked out that, across the UK, there are in the region of 628,000 families who are potentially eligible for support. Of these, 14,000 are in Northern Ireland, 29,000 in Scotland, 559,000 in England and 26,000 in Wales. Between 2020 and 2021 only a small per centage of potentially eligible families were helped by Family Fund across the UK, which provides some indication of the size of the challenge. If you add to this that a half of potentially eligible families in the UK consist of single parent families, where, as we have seen, levels of income are often lower than two parent families, it is possible to see that Family Fund's work is far from completed.

What next?

In 50 years, Family Fund has come a considerable distance from the founder Trustees' belief that there were probably about 100,000 families who would prove eligible for funding. Today, the level of support needed by families outstrips the available funding by some distance.

So what, given the progress of Family Fund during the last 50 years, are we likely to see in the next half century? The staff member who scribed details of that very first grant in the brand new ledger could scarcely have imagined where it would all lead. The Joseph Rowntree Trustees' cautious acceptance of what must initially have sometimes felt like a poisoned chalice, has proved a wise judgement. What we know is that the need will continue to be there. As we have seen earlier, there are some worrying increases in the amount of mental health difficulties experienced by young people and exponential rises in conditions like autism or Asperger's syndrome. With the huge steps forward in caring for premature babies there has been an increase in the amount of later childhood disability. At the same time with the considerable financial problems facing the UK, there is little appetite for a fundamental overhaul of the welfare benefits system which would, in turn, result in a comprehensive service for disabled children. Quite the opposite, in fact, and with further austerity will come increased challenges for families with disabled children who are struggling to pay fuel or food bills, regardless of any extras.

But what is equally sure is the resilience of the families, determined to do the best for their children and provide them with the same range of experiences that others have. Nowhere is this shown more strongly than in the accounts of family holidays, made possible through Family Fund grants. For the families these breaks not only provided the opportunity to do things together but to make the kind of permanent memories that others take for granted. There is, furthermore, an inherent irony in the way we deliver services for families with disabled children that on top of all the day-to-day challenges they have to face, they have to fight far harder than other families for services and support that by rights should be readily available.

Technology will undoubtedly continue to open up new opportunities, as computers have done. It is highly likely, therefore, given the track record and continued funding, that Family Fund will continue to find new ways to meet children's needs. Just as Family Fund was quick to seize on the importance of iPads, both as educational and entertainment tools, so too they will continue to explore how technology can better meet the needs of children with disabilities. Provided additional funding can be found, Family Fund will continue to explore the kinds of projects that support the team around the child: whether this is help for siblings or recognition of the role grandparents play in supporting families. It could also be that Family Fund will become an even more vital broker, helping families to obtain extra help through a wide range of other organisations and agencies. Such initiatives will doubtless spring from listening to what families say they need.

At various stages during its half century, Family Fund has evolved from being solely a grant maker to also acting as influencer, provider of additional services and challenger of the status quo. Finding ways of advocating long-term solutions became as vital as the individual help which was provided through grants. With an unequalled database and annual contact with thousands of families there are few organisations that can speak with such authority. In tracing fifty years of family voices, it is appropriate that the last words should go to families themselves.

Fifteen-year-old Martin is deaf. He was doing his GCSE qualifications but needed additional support to get him through his schooling. Part of this additional support included a PC to help him with his homework. Family Fund was able to provide that, alongside helping the family with a grant towards a no doubt much needed family holiday. As Martin's mum said:

"This is the only organisation that has helped us quickly and hasn't taken a lifetime to provide support. When Family Fund understood the importance of the help to Martin, it arrived promptly."

Or, as another carer recorded:

"The Fund's somebody you can turn to – they're like a rock behind you."

Bibliography

A Review of the Family Fund. Palmer S, Gibbs M and Guitard S, 1993, Management Consultancy Unit.

After Age 16 – What Next? Services and benefits for young disabled people. Hirst M and Glendinning C, 1984, Joseph Rowntree Foundation, York, ISBN 1-872470-34-3.

All Together Better. A guide for families of a disabled child with complex health care needs. Watson D, Lewis M, Townsley R, Abbott D and Cowen A, 2004, Norah Fry Research Centre and Family Fund. ISBN 0-953607803.

An Equal Recovery. Consultation by the Treasury Committee, 2022. Details available online at: An Equal Recovery – Committees – UK Parliament.

Children and Young People Strategy. Initial 3-year Delivery Plan 2021–2024. Department of Education, 2021, London. Available online at: Children and Young People's Strategy Initial 3-year Delivery Plan 2021–2024 Consultation – NI Direct – Citizen Space.

Counting the Costs of Cancer: The financial impact of cancer on children, young people and their families. Gravestock H, McDowell K, Vale D, 2011, CLIC Sargent. Available online at: Counting-the-costs-of-cancer-report.pdf (younglivesvscancer.org.uk).

Do Siblings Matter Too? Family Fund and University of Portsmouth, 2015, Family Fund. Siblings-Matter-Too-research-report.pdf (familyfund.org.uk).

Ending the Need for Food Banks: A draft national plan, 2021. Scottish Government Consultation Paper. ISBN 9781802015119.

Evaluation of the Voluntary, Community and Social Enterprise Covid-19 emergency fund package. Final Report. Department for Digital, Culture, Media and Sport, 2022.

Independent Assessment of the Efficiency of the Family Fund, 1985, Korda and Co.

My Paper Chase. True Stories of Vanished Times, an autobiography. Evans H, 2009, Little Brown Book Group, London. ISBN 978-0-349-122458.

Private Philanthropy and Public Welfare. The Joseph Rowntree Memorial Trust 1954–1979. Waddilove L, 1983, George Allen and Unwin, London. ISBN 0-04-99020064.

Report of the Committee of Enquiry into the Education of Handicapped Children and Young People. Chair: Mary Warnock, 1978, Cmnd 7212.

Report to the Secretary of State on the Lamb Inquiry Review of SEN and Disability Information. Lamb B, 2009, DCSF Publications, ISBN 978-1-84775-598-8.

Review of the Family Fund Trust. Final Report, 1999, Department of Health.

Review of the Family Fund, 2013, The Moorhouse Consortium.

SEND Review: Right support, right place, right time. Government Consultation on the SEND and alternative provision system in England, Department for Education, 2022. Green Paper, CP 624.

Shaping Children's Services. Hanvey C, 2019, Routledge, Abingdon, ISBN 978-0-8153-7464-0.

Taking Care. Cowen A, Joseph Rowntree Foundation, 1994, York. ISBN 1-872470-95-5.

Thalidomide Children, The Cohen Committee. HC Deb, 29 November 1972, vol 847, cc432–510.

The Children and Families Act 2014. Department for Education.

The DHSS/Rowntree Family Fund as an Innovation in Quasi-Government Relations. Bradshaw J, 1979, University of York Social Policy Research Unit. Paper for the PAC Conference, University of York.

The Family Fund and How it Helps. Barnes E, 1980, Joseph Rowntree Foundation, York. ISBN 1-872470-33-5.

The Family Fund. An initiative in social policy. Bradshaw J, 1980, Routledge and Kegan Paul, London. ISBN 0-7100-0520-2.

Wales Index of Multiple Deprivation Child Index Research. Bowen K and Kassa C, 2012, Contact a Family and the Family Fund.

What Do We Know About the Current Numbers of Disabled Children In England? 2022, Disabled Children's Partnership publication.

Winter Heating Benefits: Low income winter heating assistance. Consultation by the Scottish Government (2021/22) More information available online at: consult.gov.scot/social-security/winter-heating-benefits/